MW01526688

NAVIGATING BRAND SUCCESS

AMPLIFYING COMPANY GROWTH THROUGH CRUISE EVENTS

KEITH LEFKOF, ECC, TAE

Cruise Retreat Book Trilogy
www.CruiseRetreatBooks.com

Land N Sea Trips Publishing

ISBN: (paperback)
ISBN: (ebook)

TABLE OF CONTENTS

FOREWORD

When founder Samuel Cunard won the contract to deliver the Royal Mail between England and North America in 1840, the company's stage was set for the next 185 years. Cunard is renowned for innovation, many "at sea" firsts, being on the forefront of world events, holding a special relationship with Great Britain's Royal Family, and setting our signature and timeless tone for elegance, style, and the most coveted luxury ocean travel experience.

As vice president of Sales for Cunard in North America, I am honored and privileged to play a part in Cunard's enduring legacy. I always tell people that when one steps aboard a Cunard Queen, they instantly become part of the fabric of our storied history. I love introducing guests to our distinctive experience and greatly enjoy seeing how they embrace Cunard for themselves.

Perhaps the most illustrious of our voyage experiences is the iconic Transatlantic Crossing. Queen Mary 2, the flagship of the current Cunard fleet, holds the distinction of being the only ocean liner sailing regularly scheduled transatlantic crossings between New York and Southampton, England.

With so much history in the foundation of this coveted journey, this singular voyage epitomizes the essence of the Cunard experience captures the imagination, and provides inspiration like no other. Those who love traveling on a Transatlantic Crossing enjoy seven uninterrupted days at sea across the Atlantic, relish in the opportunity to unplug from everyday life to pursue creative endeavors and relax in Cunard's signature style and luxury.

The resonance of the Crossing plays out for guests in many ways: the journey can convey a deep connection with their forebears who may have sailed to Ellis Island on a Cunard ship as they left an old world for the new one; for others, it's the connection to relatives who served during WWII on either the Queen Mary or the Queen Elizabeth, which were commissioned as troop ships, and about whom Winston Churchill credited Cunard for ending the war one year early. For others, it's the dazzling glamour and luxe style enjoyed during an Atlantic voyage, finding inspiration from the many luminaries who have sailed before: from Elizabeth Taylor and Cary Grant during the "Golden Age of Travel" to today's stars such as Alan Cumming, Ed Sheeran, Wes Anderson, and Tilda Swinton, to name only a few.

In addition to pioneering the Transatlantic Crossing, Cunard has also sailed the World Voyage for more than one hundred years, starting in 1922 with the line's Laconia.

Flash forward to Cunard's newest ship. The Queen Anne, having made her debut in the spring of 2024, is the company's first ship in fourteen years. With her cutting-edge design, focus on varied and emerging art throughout the ship, elevated and expanded culinary offerings, and more diverse, compelling, and layered entertainment experiences, Queen Anne perfectly exemplifies the balance between Cunard's heritage and the forward vision we have for the company into the 21st century.

We live in a world defined by casualness but also by immediate response, 24-hour demands on our time, and information overload.

On board a Cunard ship, guests embrace the art of slowing down and the luxury of time. They rediscover the joy of dressing up, the tradition of making dinner an event, and the timeless appeal of our unique experience, which never goes out of style.

Luxury cruise brands stand out by offering passengers a travel experience that they cannot get anywhere else. At Cunard we offer "only on Cunard" experiences that offer guests the opportunity to meet and mingle with notable experts in an array of fields.

Cunard's research shows that our guests care deeply about learning, enrichment, and having new experiences. Whether it's a Q&A with celebrities such as Alan Cumming, or a lecture on exploration with maritime archaeologist Mensun Bound, Cunard is upping the ante on luxury by wowing guests. These types of programs give passengers bragging rights and provide access to experiences they wouldn't be able to find anywhere else.

For those who want to take a deep dive into their passion (or explore a new one), among my favorite Cunard experiences are our Event Voyages, which feature specific themes. These cruises provide guests an opportunity to learn from top experts in their respective fields, such as fashion designers, prima ballerinas, best-selling authors, artists, Broadway theater stars, and more.

In addition, Cunard and its iconic fleet are no strangers to hosting exciting and lavish onboard events. Many high-profile entertainers have performed onboard, and in 2017, Queen Mary 2 played hostess to the world premiere of the 20th Century FOX production of "The Greatest Showman," with stars Hugh Jackman, Zac Efron, and Zendaya gracing the ship with red carpet arrivals and screening of the popular film.

My passion for representing Cunard never dims and continues to grow. It is gratifying to be part of a luxury heritage cruise company that exemplifies foundational signature experiences blending seamlessly with creative innovation and today's luxury ethos.

From our first Atlantic Crossing 185 years ago to pioneering the first World Voyage in 1922 to our many itineraries throughout the globe, we relish sailing the world's oceans and bringing new guests aboard a Cunard ocean journey. And now I am elated that Cunard is increasing its presence in North America with another of our iconic vessels, Queen Elizabeth, homeporting for her maiden Caribbean season from Miami this year.

We who are lucky enough to work in this industry are indeed fortunate. We have the ongoing opportunity to captivate both returning and new guests to the truly unparalleled world of cruising. This type of travel brings people closer together, provides opportunities for new friendships with people from every walk of life, and provides enrichment that is singular to ocean travel.

I am grateful that I can showcase our iconic ships to the world, sparking endless inspiration, memories, and unforgettable experiences.

Jamie Paiko
Vice President of Sales
Cunard North America

INTRODUCTION

In branding, powerful symbols resonate far beyond their visual appeal, and they convey values, ignite connections, and inspire loyalty. The cover of *Navigating Brand Success* encapsulates this transformative power, blending the iconic imagery of the Statue of Liberty, the New York City skyline, and Cunard. These symbols serve as a visual metaphor for the journey every brand must undertake to achieve meaningful growth, amplified through the unique and transformative platform of cruise events. This depiction is not just about the visuals but about the potential for your brand to command attention and leave an enduring impact.

The harbor comes alive as the sun dips below the horizon, casting a golden glow over the Statue of Liberty. She stands resolute, her torch lighting the way for travelers and dreamers alike, embodying freedom, vision, and an unwavering sense of purpose. Behind her, the New York City skyline stretches upward, its towers gleaming with ambition, innovation, and endless possibilities. Cutting smoothly through the waters, a Cunard Cruise liner approaches, blending timeless elegance with modern sophistication, a floating symbol of adaptability, luxury, and enduring legacy. Together, these icons tell a story, not just of a city or a journey, but of what it takes to build a brand that stands the test of time.

This is the world of *Navigating Brand Success*, a book that invites you to reimagine branding as more than a collection of strategies or visual elements. Branding, like these landmarks, is about values, connection, and resonance. It's about crafting an experience that lingers in the hearts and minds of your audience long after the initial encounter. Through the lens of cruise events, this book explores how brands can rise above the noise, inspire loyalty, and create an immersive experience that will endure for years to come.

The Statue of Liberty is more than a monument; she is a symbol of authenticity and resilience, two qualities every brand must possess. Her presence is a reminder that the most influential brands remain true to their mission, even as they evolve to meet the demands of a changing world. Just as she welcomes all with open arms, an effective brand builds trust and fosters inclusivity, creating a sense of belonging that transcends the product or service it offers.

The New York City skyline, ever-changing and ever-inspiring, reflects the hustle and ingenuity required to thrive in competitive markets. A brand like this city must be dynamic, bold, and unafraid to reinvent itself while staying true to its core identity. The skyline's towering presence is a metaphor for the ambition every brand must embrace, namely, a willingness to reach higher, dream bigger, and adapt creatively to challenges.

Completing this iconic trio is the storied legacy of Cunard Cruises, an enduring symbol of luxury, heritage, and adaptability. For over a century, Cunard has navigated changing waters while preserving its essence, delivering exceptional experiences that remain synonymous with its name. As their ships sail past the Statue of Liberty and into New York Harbor, they remind us that brand success requires a delicate balance: honoring one's roots while continuously innovating to meet evolving expectations. Cunard's journey exemplifies how to sustain relevance without losing sight of identity, a vital lesson for any brand striving to build a legacy.

These icons, Lady Liberty, the New York skyline, and Cunard Cruises, are more than imagery on the cover of this book. They symbolize the profound principles that elevate a brand from a name to an enduring legacy. They set the stage for a journey into the art and science of branding through the transformative power of cruise events.

Picture a brainstorming session on the deck of a luxury liner, the ocean stretching endlessly around you. Envision networking dinners beneath the stars, conversations flowing as naturally as the waves. Imagine team-building activities on pristine, secluded shores, where the distractions of daily life melt away, replaced by authentic connection and shared purpose. Cruise events are not just meetings; they are immersive experiences that raise your brand with the qualities of luxury, adventure, possibility, and most importantly, fun for all attendees and management.

Hosting a cruise event sends a clear message: your brand values excellence, creativity, and connection. It positions your business as innovative, forward-thinking, and deeply invested in delivering unforgettable moments. Onboard, relationships are forged, ideas are born, and stories are created stories that elevate your brand far beyond the confines of a logo or tagline.

In these pages, you'll embark on a journey to uncover what makes a brand more than just a name. You'll discover how cruise events offer a unique opportunity to amplify your message, forge unforgettable connections, and create lasting impact. Just as Cunard Cruises blends luxury with legacy, New York combines hustle with heart, or the Statue of Liberty radiates purpose with resilience, this book shows you how to craft a brand that stands tall, adapts, and inspires. Cruise events offer an unparalleled opportunity to engage your audience on a deeper level.

A cruise isn't just a venue; it's a statement. It tells your audience that your brand values connection, experience, and excellence. And when your message is delivered with the ocean as your stage and iconic landmarks as your co-stars, it doesn't just resonate; it inspires. Hosting a cruise event is more than a strategy; it's an opportunity to elevate your brand to new heights, turning every wave into a ripple of impact that reaches far beyond the ship's deck.

Navigating Brand Success is your guide to harnessing these opportunities. It's a call to see your brand as a legacy in the making, a chance to inspire not just recognition but loyalty and passion. This is more than a book; it's an invitation to rethink what your brand can be.

The journey begins here; step aboard and discover the endless possibilities that await.

1

THE ALLURE OF THE SEAS: REIMAGINING CORPORATE BRANDING THROUGH CRUISE EVENTS

In today's dynamic corporate landscape, businesses are constantly seeking groundbreaking strategies to inspire, re-engage, and drive their teams to new heights. Among the innovative approaches emerging, hosting a corporate conference aboard a luxury cruise ship stands out as a truly transformative experience that redefines the traditional event setting.

Are you still hosting traditional, old-school conferences in 2025 to promote your transformational brand? The kind where your attendees are packed into a stuffy hotel ballroom, disengaged, distracted, and counting the hours until the next coffee break? The cruise-based conference offers a solution to this fatigue by elevating the experience with the open sea, breathtaking views, and unforgettable destinations.

Have you ever considered an Alaskan cruise as the backdrop for your next conference? Envision this - Your cruise ship gracefully gliding through the majestic Inside Passage, your attendees surrounded by glaciers, towering mountains, and the vibrant wildlife of the Pacific Northwest. Each day brings new sights: icebergs, humpback whales breaching, and eagles soaring against a pristine blue sky.

This awe-inspiring setting is more than just a stunning backdrop. It's a powerful catalyst for innovation. It sparks creative thinking, fosters meaningful collaboration, and transforms the ordinary into the extraordinary. It's not just a conference; it's an unforgettable experience that recharges your attendees, fuels their inspiration, and propels your brand to new heights.

Picture courtesy of Royal Caribbean International

Craving a warmer, more vibrant setting?

Imagine hosting your event in the Caribbean, where every destination exudes energy, vibrancy, and relaxation. A sun-kissed environment not only lifts spirits but also enhances focus and creativity, making it the perfect setting to engage and inspire your attendees. Elevate the experience by including Royal Caribbean's exclusive Bahamas private island, Perfect Day at CocoCay, or their brand-new private island, The Royal Beach Club at Paradise Island in Nassau, Bahamas, which is opening in Q4 2025, in your itinerary. These exclusive experiences are only available through Royal Caribbean and Celebrity Cruises.

Picture your team basking in the tropical sunshine as they enjoy one-of-a-kind experiences tailored to both adventure and relaxation. Energize the group with thrilling activities like conquering North America's tallest waterslide or floating high above the island in a helium balloon, taking in breathtaking views. For those seeking a more serene escape, imagine team members unwinding in overwater cabanas, sipping refreshing drinks while the turquoise waters lap gently beneath them.

Perfect Day at CocoCay offers the ideal blend of excitement and tranquility, fostering connections and team bonding like no other venue. Whether your attendees are snorkeling vibrant coral reefs, networking by the largest freshwater pool in the Caribbean, or simply soaking up the sun on pristine beaches, the setting invigorates their senses and enhances their experience.

Does your group seek an exclusive, adults-only oasis to elevate your next event?

Step into the refined elegance of Hideaway Beach, the secluded adults-only escape at Perfect Day at CocoCay. This private haven redefines sophistication, blending relaxation and vibrancy to create the ultimate environment for your brand to captivate and connect.

Picture your attendees reclining in luxurious cabanas with panoramic views of turquoise waters, engaging in meaningful conversations by the infinity pool, or savoring signature cocktails crafted by expert mixologists at the full-service bar. Every detail of Hideaway Beach radiates exclusivity and style, offering a setting where connections flourish and ideas flow effortlessly.

This serene retreat provides the perfect canvas for intimate gatherings, team-building activities, or branded experiences that leave an indelible mark. Whether hosting a networking social by the pool, organizing a wellness session under swaying palm trees, or curating a bespoke experience designed for your group, Hideaway Beach elevates your event from ordinary to unforgettable.

Here, every moment is infused with luxury and purpose, ensuring your attendees feel valued and inspired. Hideaway Beach is an immersive experience, a place where creativity thrives, connections deepen, and your brand becomes part of an extraordinary story of connection and innovation.

This is the essence of Navigating Brand Success, a fresh paradigm shift that propels corporate events into an engaging, 21st-century experience aboard world-class cruise ships to enhance your branding and immersive image.

Picture courtesy of Royal Caribbean International

THE TRANSFORMATIVE POWER OF THE CRUISE CONFERENCE EXPERIENCE

The cruise conference experience is an innovative, transformative approach to corporate gatherings, redefining what it means to bring teams together, inspire creativity, and promote a brand. As businesses navigate today's dynamic landscape, a fresh alternative to conventional conferences has emerged, allowing companies to not only re-engage their teams but also elevate their brand image in a seamless, immersive environment. Hosting a conference aboard a luxury cruise ship is more than just an event; it's a journey that aligns professional growth with rejuvenation, blending work with relaxation in a way that leaves a lasting impact on every attendee.

Imagine exchanging the familiar confines of a hotel ballroom for the endless horizon of the open sea. Aboard a five-star cruise ship, conference organizers no longer need to juggle the logistics of separate venues, transportation, dining, and entertainment. Cruise packages offer all-inclusive convenience, encompassing everything from luxurious accommodations and gourmet dining to state-of-the-art meeting spaces and leisure activities, which streamlines event planning and eliminates stress for organizers. Every detail, from elegant meeting rooms to cutting-edge AV technology and diverse dining options, is thoughtfully designed and coordinated, allowing the conference to flow effortlessly. The attendees, in turn, can focus on what matters most: engaging with the content, building connections, and fully immersing themselves in the experience.

This unique setting amplifies networking and team-building opportunities in ways that traditional events simply cannot match. Picture your team connecting over an Alaskan adventure, with glaciers and soaring mountains as a dramatic backdrop, or bonding on a sunlit Caribbean deck after a snorkeling excursion. With each day bringing a new destination, such as cliff-diving in turquoise waters, exploring cultural sites, or zip-lining through lush rainforests, teams forge stronger bonds and shared memories that foster greater unity and collaboration. Networking unfolds naturally in this relaxed, inspiring environment, whether over a shared adventure or a casual dinner at sea. The traditional barriers between work and play dissolve as each destination becomes a unique catalyst for creativity, conversation, and collaboration, creating moments that resonate long after the voyage ends.

A cruise-based conference also embodies a forward-thinking approach to employee engagement, sending a powerful message about the company's commitment to innovation and the well-being of its team. By investing in an event that allows employees to learn, relax, and explore, leaders demonstrate an understanding that rejuvenated employees bring fresh energy and productivity to their roles. When conference sessions are paired with breathtaking experiences witnessing the northern lights in Alaska, discovering vibrant island cultures in the Caribbean, or even just taking in an evening under starlit skies teams feel valued and motivated, leading to increased loyalty and a shared enthusiasm for the company's mission.

The power of place in this setting also transforms the event into an unparalleled branding opportunity. The open sea and high-end amenities of a luxury cruise create a backdrop for corporate storytelling that is as captivating as it is memorable. Imagine unveiling a new product against the panoramic expanse of the ocean or conducting team workshops in an environment where each day's adventure reflects the brand's values and aspirations. This setting naturally elevates the brand, aligning it with qualities of innovation, luxury, and forward-thinking while fostering an emotional connection that endures.

Imagine stepping aboard a luxury cruise ship where every detail of your conference has been meticulously planned and seamlessly executed. From the moment you embark, the all-inclusive nature of a cruise ship conference ensures an effortless experience for both organizers and attendees. Gourmet dining, luxurious accommodations, state-of-the-art meeting spaces, and world-class entertainment are all integrated into one cohesive package, creating a floating venue where every interaction feels intentional and every moment meaningful.

For organizers, this streamlined approach means spending less time buried in logistical complexities and more time focusing on the elements that truly make the event impactful, such as engaging content, dynamic networking opportunities, and meaningful experiences. For attendees, the convenience of having everything within walking distance fosters an intimate and immersive environment. Whether it's attending a breakout session in a cutting-edge conference room, enjoying a casual networking lunch on the deck, or bonding with colleagues during an off-ship excursion, the ease of access and thoughtful curation enables a seamless blend of learning and leisure.

The cruise ship itself becomes a self-contained conference center, offering amenities that go far beyond what traditional land-based venues can provide. This inherent structure represents a more innovative, more efficient approach to event planning, often yielding approximately 30% savings compared to a comparable five-star hotel conference. The all-inclusive pricing model encompasses everything: accommodations, diverse dining options, complimentary conference facilities equipped with advanced audiovisual technology, and even Broadway-style shows, live music, and comedic performances. By consolidating these elements under one roof, cruise conferences eliminate the hidden costs and logistical headaches that frequently accompany traditional venues.

This cost-effective clarity allows organizations to focus their budgets and energy on creating a memorable and transformative event. The predictable expenses and comprehensive offerings free planners to craft an experience that reflects the company's values and aspirations while maximizing return on investment.

Choosing to host a conference on a cruise ship is more than just a logistical decision; it's a bold statement of innovation, creativity, and employee engagement. It reflects a commitment to creating a space where professional development and personal connection intersect in a meaningful way. The unique setting of the open seas becomes a powerful platform for brand storytelling, where every element from curated experiences to scenic backdrops works in harmony to reinforce the company's vision and inspire attendees.

As companies strive to stand out in an increasingly competitive marketplace, cruise conferences offer a clear advantage: a powerful synergy between place and purpose. By navigating their brand's success on the high seas, organizations embark on a journey that celebrates adventure, fosters creativity, and promotes growth. A cruise conference is a voyage of transformation where traditional boundaries dissolve, and a new era of engagement, inspiration, and enduring connections begins.

2

THE EVOLUTION OF EVENT BRANDING AND THE FUTURE OF BRANDING

In today's hyper-connected, experience-driven marketplace, brands are more than logos or catchy taglines; they are dynamic, living identities that resonate with consumers on emotional, intellectual, and sensory levels. This transformation has led to the rise of event branding, a powerful strategy that extends a brand's influence by crafting immersive experiences. It brings a brand's values, story, and identity to life in a memorable way. As we explore event branding and envision its future, we'll see that this is an approach designed to capture attention and create lasting connections, fostering loyalty and engagement like never before.

WHAT IS EVENT BRANDING?

Event branding is the strategic process of infusing a brand's personality, values, and goals into an event, making every aspect of it, from the venue and décor to the speakers and activities, an authentic extension of the brand. Unlike traditional advertising or digital campaigns, event branding creates an immersive, hands-on experience, inviting participants to interact with the brand in a meaningful and memorable way. It turns attendees into active participants, allowing them to live the brand through their senses and emotions rather than simply observing it.

Imagine a tech company hosting a conference that showcases the latest innovations through interactive displays, workshops, and immersive technology like VR and AR. Attendees don't just hear about the brand's cutting-edge products; they experience them firsthand. Or consider a wellness brand hosting a retreat, where every activity, from the yoga sessions and meditation spaces to the food served, reflects its commitment to health, balance, and holistic living. This is the power of event branding: it transforms the audience from passive viewers to engaged participants, allowing the brand's essence to resonate on a deeper level.

THE PURPOSE AND POWER OF EVENT BRANDING

The main goal of event branding is to foster a memorable connection between the brand and its audience. When done effectively, event branding creates an environment that is not only memorable but also aligns with the brand's identity, helping to build trust and loyalty. Event branding achieves three key objectives:

1. **Deepening Brand Engagement**: A well-branded event brings a brand to life, inviting attendees to engage with it in real, tangible ways. This level of engagement fosters a connection that traditional media cannot match.

2. **Amplifying Brand Awareness**: Events are social experiences, both in-person and online. With attendees sharing their experiences on social media, branded events generate organic exposure, reaching new audiences and amplifying brand awareness.

3. **Building Loyalty Through Experience**: Attendees who feel a personal connection to a brand are more likely to become loyal customers. By creating an environment that aligns with attendees' values and interests, brands foster a sense of belonging, which translates into long-term loyalty.

Photo Courtesy of Regent Seven Seas

THE FUTURE OF BRANDING: WHERE ARE WE HEADING?

As we look to the future, branding continues to evolve in response to changing consumer expectations, technological advancements, and a growing emphasis on authenticity and personalization. Here's where we're headed:

1. Experience-Centric Branding

As audiences crave more meaningful and immersive interactions, brands are evolving to create experiences that engage all the senses. The future of branding lies in curating multi-dimensional experiences that go beyond visual identity and advertising. These experiences connect with consumers on a deeper level, leaving an indelible mark. Brands will increasingly invest in live events, pop-up experiences, and branded spaces, transforming their interactions into moments that evoke emotion and create lasting memories.

2. Integration of Advanced Technology

Technology is reshaping how brands connect with audiences. In the future, branding will increasingly leverage augmented reality (AR), virtual reality (VR), and artificial intelligence (AI) to create personalized and interactive brand experiences. Imagine a virtual brand event where attendees from anywhere in the world can immerse themselves in a 3D digital environment that mirrors a physical space. Or consider AI-powered personalization, where a brand tailors its messaging and offerings to each attendee's preferences in real time. This blend of physical and digital worlds will make branding more immersive, accessible, and impactful.

3. Purpose-Driven and Value-Based Branding

Today's consumers are more discerning than ever; they seek brands that stand for something beyond profits. The future of branding is purpose-driven, with companies increasingly building their brand identities around sustainability, social responsibility, and ethical practices. Event branding will reflect these values, using the platform to raise awareness, foster community, and make a positive impact. Events will become opportunities for brands to showcase their commitment to issues like environmental conservation, inclusivity, and social justice, creating connections based on shared values.

4. Personalization at Scale

Consumers expect personalization, and the future of branding will deliver it at scale. With data and AI-driven insights, brands will be able to craft experiences that are uniquely tailored to each individual. Personalized invitations, exclusive content, and custom interactions will make attendees feel valued and understood. Event branding, too, will evolve to allow for more customized interactions, whether through curated breakout sessions, tailored workshops, or exclusive experiences designed to appeal to each attendee's unique interests.

5. Emphasis on Community Building

Brands are increasingly viewed as communities rather than just product providers. The future of branding will focus on fostering communities around shared passions, lifestyles, or goals. Event branding will play a key role in creating these communities, offering a physical or virtual space where individuals can connect over a shared identity or purpose. By positioning themselves as facilitators of these communities, brands can build stronger, more meaningful relationships with their audience.

EMBRACING THE FUTURE: STRATEGIES FOR EFFECTIVE EVENT BRANDING

To successfully navigate this future of branding, companies need to adopt innovative strategies for their events. Here are a few approaches that can help:

1. **Curate Unique Experiences**: Make every detail of the event align with the brand's identity. From the location and décor to the activities and speaker lineup, every element should serve as a brand touchpoint, creating a cohesive and immersive experience.
2. **Leverage Interactive Technologies**: Use AR, VR, and AI to make the event interactive and engaging. Allow attendees to experience the brand's products and values firsthand, transforming abstract concepts into tangible experiences.

3. **Promote Authentic Connections**: Authenticity is paramount. Encourage real, meaningful interactions by designing event activities that foster connection and collaboration among attendees. The focus should be on creating genuine bonds rather than purely transactional encounters.

4. **Incorporate Values and Purpose**: Reflect the brand's values throughout the event. From sustainable practices to socially conscious themes, let the event demonstrate the brand's commitment to important issues, fostering connections based on shared values.

5. **Offer Personalized Experiences**: Personalize the event experience wherever possible, using attendee data to curate content, activities, and messaging. Make each attendee feel valued and create a unique journey that resonates with them personally.

THE FUTURE IS EXPERIENTIAL AND IMMERSIVE

Branding today is evolving into a journey of deeper connections, rich experiences, and meaningful engagement. As we move forward, experiential events will be at the forefront of this transformation, allowing brands to craft immersive experiences that foster lasting emotional bonds. With advances in technology driving more personalization and interactivity and with audiences seeking authenticity and purpose, future branding will be defined by experiences that are not just memorable but genuinely meaningful.

Event branding is no longer just about creating memorable occasions; it's about crafting immersive moments that resonate deeply, inspiring loyalty, fostering community, and cultivating a shared sense of purpose. Cruise-based conferences and events answer this demand, offering an environment that transcends the limitations of traditional venues. They immerse participants in an experience that combines work, adventure, and connection, uniquely blending professional growth with personal exploration in stunning settings.

The brands that embrace this evolution will be those that not only adapt but lead, thriving in an era where connection is paramount. They will guide the way in a world where the strongest brands are those that evoke genuine emotion, spark engagement, and build a sense of belonging. For these brands, experiential events like cruise-based conferences are the future of powerful, immersive branding.

3

ANCHORING CORPORATE SUCCESS: HOW EVENT BRANDING DRIVES CORPORATE GROWTH

In today's competitive marketplace, brands are no longer static logos or abstract concepts; they are living, breathing experiences that create lasting emotional connections with audiences. This evolution has brought event branding to the forefront as a critical strategy for corporate success. When companies infuse their brand into every aspect of an event, they create an immersive experience that resonates on multiple levels, leaving attendees not just impressed but inspired. In this chapter, we explore the power of event branding and why it has become indispensable for companies striving to stand out, build loyalty, and grow.

Photo Courtesy of Royal Carribean International

1. Strengthens Brand Identity

At its core, event branding is about consistently reflecting a company's values, mission, and personality throughout the event experience. From the venue design and decor to the speaker lineup and activities, every element should feel like an extension of the brand. This consistency reinforces brand identity, making it easy for attendees to recognize and remember what the brand stands for. A cohesive event experience leaves attendees with a clear understanding of the brand's essence, creating a stronger connection that lasts long after the event ends.

Imagine a luxury cruise ship transformed into your brand's floating fashion haven, with sunset runway shows, pop-up boutiques, and exclusive workshops. Guests explore your collection in immersive settings, from chic onboard events to glamorous shore excursions. This unique experience strengthens emotional connections with influencers and buyers, positioning your brand as a trendsetter while amplifying awareness and loyalty in a competitive market.

2. Increases Customer Loyalty

When done well, event branding doesn't just showcase the brand; attendees feel aligned with the brand. Immersive experiences foster emotional connections, which are key to building loyalty. A well-branded event that aligns with attendees' interests and values will resonate deeply, creating a lasting relationship between the audience and the brand.

Transform a luxury cruise ship into an interactive hub for your real estate brand, blending collaboration and fun. Engage clients with immersive workshops, team-building activities, and virtual property tours. Add networking mixers, wine tastings, and wellness sessions to create unforgettable experiences. This dynamic fusion of business and leisure strengthens relationships, reinforces your brand, and leaves a lasting impression.

3. Boosts Employee Engagement

Event branding is not only for external audiences. Internally branded events have the power to energize employees, aligning them with the company's mission and fostering a sense of pride and belonging. When employees see the brand brought to life in a meaningful way, their connection to the company is reinforced, and their motivation to contribute to its success is strengthened. Consider a corporate retreat where every element, from team-building exercises to branded merchandise, reflects the company's culture and values. This experience fosters camaraderie, enhances team spirit, and boosts morale, creating a more engaged and productive workforce that's aligned with the brand's vision.

4. Enhances Brand Awareness

One of the biggest advantages of event branding is the potential for increased brand awareness. A well-branded event attracts attention, drawing in new audiences who might not have otherwise encountered the brand. These events act as a powerful introduction, presenting the brand in a memorable, impactful way that resonates beyond the confines of traditional advertising.

For instance, a food and beverage company hosting a tasting event not only showcases its products but also attracts attendees who may share their experience with friends or on social media. This organic exposure extends the brand's reach, generating awareness among potential new customers.

5. Drives Organic Word-of-Mouth

A uniquely branded event gives attendees something worth talking about, encouraging them to share their experiences with their networks. From social media posts and photos to stories shared with friends, branded events generate word-of-mouth marketing that's more trusted and engaging than paid ads. The excitement and authenticity of these shares amplify the brand's visibility and credibility.

Consider a travel brand hosting an adventure-themed event that includes immersive VR experiences of exotic destinations. Attendees are likely to post about their experiences, sharing the excitement with friends and followers. Each post extends the brand's reach, driving organic buzz and encouraging others to explore the brand.

6. Differentiates from Competitors

In crowded markets, differentiation is essential. A well-branded event helps a company stand out by showcasing unique qualities that make it different from competitors. When attendees can see, feel, and experience what sets the brand apart, it builds a lasting impression that distinguishes the brand in their minds.

For example, if two tech companies host events, the one that integrates its branding in innovative ways, such as through interactive demonstrations, futuristic displays, and personalized tech experiences will leave a stronger impression. This differentiated experience positions the brand as memorable and distinctive, which is crucial in competitive markets.

7. Builds Trust and Credibility

Consistent and professional event branding conveys reliability and authority, helping to build trust and credibility among attendees. A well-executed event demonstrates the company's attention to detail, commitment to quality, and understanding of its audience's needs, all of which contribute to a trustworthy brand image.

Picture a financial services company hosting a branded seminar where every session, speaker, and handout is meticulously designed to reflect professionalism and expertise. Such an event assures attendees of the company's reliability and trustworthiness, fostering confidence in the brand.

8. Encourages Brand Advocacy

When attendees have a positive, meaningful experience, they're more likely to become advocates for the brand, promoting it within their networks. This advocacy extends the event's impact as attendees share their experiences and recommend the brand to others, essentially becoming brand ambassadors.

Imagine a fashion brand hosting a pop-up event where attendees can preview and try out a new collection. If the event is enjoyable, attendees will likely tell their friends, post on social media, and bring the brand into conversations, amplifying its reach and influence.

9. Increases ROI on Events

Investing in event branding can significantly improve the return on investment. A branded event attracts more engaged participants, leading to better outcomes such as conversions, partnerships, and increased revenue. When the event aligns with the brand's objectives and resonates with the audience, it becomes more than just an expenditure; it becomes a valuable tool for growth.

A technology company might host a branded conference showcasing its latest innovations. This event could result in new business partnerships, product sales, or media coverage, all outcomes that contribute to a higher ROI by directly impacting the brand's growth.

10. Creates Lasting Connections

Perhaps the most powerful aspect of event branding is its ability to create lasting connections. Events that reflect the brand's values and personality create a unique, memorable experience that deepens relationships with clients, partners, and employees alike. These connections support long-term success, as attendees carry their positive impressions and associations with them long after the event concludes.

A nonprofit organization, for instance, might host a gala event that highlights its mission, values, and impact on the community. Attendees who connect emotionally with the event's purpose are more likely to stay engaged with the organization, supporting its initiatives and contributing to its long-term success.

Photo Courtesy of Cunard

EVENT BRANDING AS A CATALYST FOR CORPORATE GROWTH

Event branding is a strategic tool that goes beyond aesthetics to create immersive experiences that reflect a brand's true identity and values. When companies invest in well-branded events, they cultivate emotional connections, foster loyalty, and enhance brand recognition. Each aspect of a branded event, from the design and decor to the activities and messaging, serves as an extension of the brand, creating an experience that resonates long after the event has ended.

As we have explored, the benefits of event branding are vast. From strengthening brand identity and increasing customer loyalty to building brand advocacy and boosting ROI, branded events have a transformative impact on corporate success. In a world where experiences matter, event branding is a powerful way for companies to not only stand out but to thrive. By creating environments that engage, inspire, and connect, companies can turn every event into a memorable journey that supports their long-term growth and success.

4

THE ART OF EVENT BRANDING

Event branding is a transformative art form that turns ordinary gatherings into dynamic extensions of a brand's identity. It's not just about coordinating visual elements or crafting a catchy tagline; it's about creating immersive experiences that allow participants to truly live the brand. Every detail, from the first invitation to the post-event follow-up, becomes a thread in a story that leaves a lasting impression on those who experience it.

Picture stepping into an event where the environment immediately captivates you. The colors reflect the brand's palette, the music resonates with its tone, and the activities perfectly align with its mission. Whether it's a tech company showcasing groundbreaking innovations through interactive demos or a wellness brand hosting a retreat steeped in balance and mindfulness, the brand's essence permeates every moment. Attendees are participants in a shared journey that goes beyond the surface and connects on an emotional, sensory, and intellectual level.

The advantages of enhancing a brand with an event are profound. Events are unique in their ability to foster emotional connections. While ads or digital campaigns might catch someone's attention, events create memories. Crafted with care, these moments build bonds that last, turning attendees into advocates and loyal customers. They also provide a stage for brands to showcase their identity and values in an authentic and tangible way. Through these experiences, brands reinforce what they stand for and differentiate themselves in a crowded marketplace.

Another remarkable power of events lies in their social nature. Attendees often share their experiences with their networks, creating a ripple effect that amplifies the brand's visibility. A branded event can spark conversations, generate buzz, and attract new audiences far beyond the venue's walls. And within those walls, brands can engage with their audience on a deeply personal level, tailoring experiences to individual interests and making participants feel genuinely seen and valued.

Beyond building connections, events serve as platforms to establish credibility. Whether through keynote speeches, interactive workshops, or product demonstrations, brands can showcase their expertise and leadership in their field. These moments not only inform but inspire trust, positioning the brand as an authority worth following.

Events also foster a sense of community, bringing together people with shared interests, values, or goals.

This sense of belonging is powerful. When attendees feel part of something bigger, a movement, or a mission, they're more likely to stay loyal and invested in the brand's journey. And the impact doesn't end when the event concludes. Through thoughtful follow-ups, exclusive content, or invitations to future experiences, brands can maintain the momentum, keeping their audience engaged and connected.

In today's world, where people crave authenticity and meaningful interactions, event branding has become essential. Consumers are no longer drawn solely by products or services; they want to connect with brands that resonate with their values and inspire them. Events provide the perfect medium for this connection, offering spaces where brands can authentically share their story and invite participants to become a part of it.

The magic of event branding lies in its ability to turn moments into movements, memories into loyalty, and attendees into lifelong advocates. It's a transformative way to create enduring relationships. For brands willing to embrace the power of experiential storytelling, the rewards are immense, creating a legacy of trust, connection, and shared purpose that stands the test of time.

THE POWER OF EVENT BRANDING: 13 REASONS IT DRIVES SUCCESS

- ❖ **Enhanced Brand Recognition:** Consistent and visually appealing branding increases brand recognition and recall among attendees.
- ❖ **Positive Perception:** Effective event branding creates a positive perception of your company, making attendees more likely to trust and engage with your brand.
- ❖ **Increased Engagement:** At events, your ideal customers can engage with your brand in a unique way and learn more about your values, products, etc.
- ❖ **ROI:** Companies investing in event branding often see a higher return on investment, with branded events driving more significant business results.
- ❖ **Memorability:** We tend to remember events, so be sure to make a positive impression that the participants will recall with joy and associate with your brand.
- ❖ **Competitive Edge:** Events are almost a superpower to gain a competitive edge over the other players in the industry if executed correctly.
- ❖ **Enhanced Sponsorship Value:** Partner up with like-minded brands to increase your reach while also creating a revenue source.
- ❖ **Social Media Amplification:** Events are likely to be shared on social media, extending your reach and visibility beyond the event itself. It also helps build a content bank.

❖ **Customer Loyalty:** Positive event experiences foster greater brand loyalty and can turn attendees into advocates for your brand.

❖ **Professional Image:** Consistent and professional branding signals quality and reliability, enhancing your company's reputation.

❖ **Experiential Marketing:** Events provide unique opportunities for experiential marketing, allowing attendees to engage with your brand in meaningful and memorable ways.

❖ **Data Collection:** Events can facilitate data collection and insights, helping you understand your audience better and refine your marketing strategies.

❖ **Sales Boost:** Engaging and well-branded events often correlate with immediate and post-event sales increases, as well as a robust pipeline of leads.

THE ELEMENTS OF EVENT BRANDING

Brand Identity - Consistently use your brand's logo, color scheme, and typography across all event materials to reinforce brand recognition.

Attendee Experience - Choose a venue and design the event space to align with your brand's image and create the desired ambiance.

Digital Presence - Develop a branded event website and app that provide essential information and enhance the user experience.

Promotional Materials - Design invitations, announcements, and name badges that are visually appealing and consistent with your brand's identity.

Interactive Elements - Use branded engagement tools like live polls and social media walls to create a participatory experience for attendees.

Post-Event Follow-Up - Send branded surveys and share event highlights to gather feedback and extend the event's impact.

ENHANCE BRAND PERCEPTION THROUGH EVENTS

All brands want to be perceived in a certain way, whether that is as kind, sophisticated, or as a budget-friendly alternative. Through strategic event branding, companies can communicate their identity, values, and vision in a way that fosters strong emotional connections and positive associations with their brand. Let's have a look at what the data says!

91% Creating Memorable Experiences: Events provide an immersive hotspot where attendees can experience the brand firsthand. A well-branded event leaves a lasting impression, making the brand more memorable. According to a study by EventTrack, 91% of consumers have more positive feelings about brands after attending events.

70% Consistency and Recognition: Consistent branding across all event elements ensures that attendees can easily recognize and remember the brand. This consistency helps reinforce the brand's identity and message. A study by WiFi Talent found that 70% of event attendees become regular customers after an experiential marketing event.

87% Showcasing Brand Values: Events offer a unique opportunity to highlight a brand's values in action. For instance, an eco-friendly company can demonstrate its commitment to sustainability through the use of green materials and practices at its events. Research by Cone Communications revealed that 87% of consumers would purchase a product because a company advocated for an issue they cared about.

EVENTS CAN HELP BRANDS STAND OUT IN A COMPETITIVE MARKET

Events can significantly help brands stand out and gain a competitive advantage by offering unique, engaging experiences that resonate with their target audience. For example, a tech company might host an exclusive product launch featuring interactive demos and augmented reality experiences, highlighting the product's unique features and leaving a lasting impression.

Direct engagement at events fosters personal connections that can be more impactful than digital advertising. A cosmetics brand, for example, can hold pop-up events for personalized beauty consultations, building trust and loyalty. Events also allow brands to showcase their latest innovation. A car manufacturer could organize an auto show highlighting the latest electric and autonomous vehicle technology, demonstrating their cutting-edge advancements.

Creating a sense of community at events enhances brand loyalty and advocacy. A fitness brand might organize local boot camps and wellness retreats, fostering a supportive community and encouraging word-of-mouth promotion. Providing exclusive access to new products or experiences can generate excitement. A fashion brand hosting a VIP pre-launch event allows top customers to preview and purchase items before the public, creating buzz and elevating the brand's status.

Immersive, sensory-rich experiences make the brand more memorable. A travel company could set up a booth where visitors explore destinations using VR technology, creating a vivid impression. Events also provide a platform for collecting direct feedback, allowing brands to understand their customers better. Additionally, they offer a concentrated opportunity to communicate key brand messages and values.

87% of C-Suite executives believe live events create a lasting connection. Source: Endless Events

74% of event attendees have a more positive opinion about a brand after an event. Source: WifiTalents

Connect Over Brand Values and Purpose

Brands breathe and live by their values. However, the values that you have worked so hard on might not have reached your target audience. Events are a perfect opportunity to show what your brand stands for and put it in the storefront for your visitors to experience. Ideally, your participants can answer the following questions or at least have some idea of the following:

Values - Who are you? What do you believe in? How do you work?

Vision - What do you aspire to achieve in the long term? Where do you see the organization in the future?

Purpose - Why do you exist? What drives you? What impact do you aim to make? 7/10 consumers say they tend to buy from brands that reflect their personal values.

EVENTS: THE GATEWAY TO CREATING LASTING BRAND EXPERIENCES

In a world driven by connection and storytelling, brands must do more than deliver products or services; they must create moments that inspire, engage, and endure. Immersive experiences hold the power to transform a brand from a name into a legacy, fostering deep emotional ties and making lasting impressions. Whether it's a secluded wine tasting in an Italian cave or a starlit safari sundowner, these experiences not only captivate attendees but also create memories that resonate long after the event.

For brands, immersive experiences provide a unique platform to connect with audiences on a deeper level. They engage the senses, evoke emotions, and align the brand with moments of joy, discovery, and wonder. Nowhere is this potential more evident than in the cruise industry, where the ability to transport attendees to stunning destinations pairs seamlessly with world-class service and curated experiences.

To create a truly impactful event, brands must focus on designing experiences that reflect their values while resonating with their audience. Immersive moments, such as those offered by cruise lines, provide the ideal setting for fostering connection and loyalty. By combining stunning locations, exclusive activities, and unparalleled service, these experiences ensure that the brand is not just remembered but cherished.

For those ready to elevate their branding strategy, look no further than the transformative power of immersive experiences. Whether it's through adventure, culture, or relaxation, these moments inspire attendees, enrich relationships, and create stories that endure for generations.

THE ROLE OF CRUISE LINES IN CREATING IMMERSIVE BRAND EXPERIENCES

Cruise lines offer a distinct advantage when it comes to hosting events. With the ability to transport guests to exotic locations while delivering exceptional onboard experiences, they create a seamless blend of adventure, culture, and relaxation.

Here's how three luxury cruise lines, Regent Seven Seas, Norwegian Cruise Line, and Cunard, excel in offering immersive experiences that transform events into unforgettable brand narratives.

REGENT SEVEN SEAS: ULTRA-LUXURY AND PERSONALIZED JOURNEYS

Regent Seven Seas Cruises redefines luxury, offering guests all-inclusive experiences tailored to their desires. Imagine hosting an intimate corporate retreat where attendees enjoy private shore excursions to some of the world's most exclusive destinations. Picture your group exploring the vineyards of Bordeaux with a private sommelier or stepping into the ancient ruins of Ephesus for a candlelit dinner under the stars.

Onboard, Regent delivers the ultimate in luxury. Brands can host events in elegantly appointed lounges or open-air decks overlooking the ocean. Attendees can enjoy curated wellness experiences at the Serene Spa & Wellness™ or participate in a bespoke culinary workshop led by a world-class chef. These experiences blend opulence with authenticity, ensuring that your brand is associated with exclusivity, excellence, and unforgettable moments.

Photo Courtesy of Regent Seven Seas

NORWEGIAN CRUISE LINE: CREATIVITY AND ADVENTURE ON THE HIGH SEAS

Norwegian Cruise Line (NCL) offers a dynamic mix of adventure and entertainment, making it ideal for brands looking to create energetic and engaging events. For example, NCL's private island, *Great Stirrup Cay*, provides a pristine tropical setting for team-building activities, water sports, and private networking sessions by the beach. Guests can relax in luxurious beachfront villas or enjoy a sunset cocktail party overlooking the crystal-clear waters.

Onboard, NCL's wide range of activities caters to diverse interests. From exhilarating go-kart races on the ship's top deck to Broadway-style performances in state-of-the-art theaters, the options for creating memorable moments are endless. Brands can also leverage NCL's culinary diversity by hosting global-themed dining experiences, where attendees can sample dishes inspired by the ship's international itinerary. These high-energy, creative settings align your brand with excitement, adventure, and innovation.

Photo Courtesy of Norwegian Cruise Lines

CUNARD: TIMELESS ELEGANCE AND CULTURAL IMMERSION

Cunard brings a sense of timeless elegance and tradition to the cruise experience, making it perfect for brands seeking sophistication and cultural depth. Events on Cunard ships, such as the legendary *Queen Mary 2*, evoke the grandeur of a bygone era while offering modern luxury. Imagine hosting a gala dinner in the iconic Queens Room, where your attendees can enjoy a black-tie evening complete with live orchestra performances and gourmet cuisine.

Cunard also excels in cultural immersion. Their transatlantic crossings often feature Enrichment Programs, where renowned speakers, authors, and artists host workshops and lectures. Brands can incorporate these elements into their events, offering attendees intellectual engagement alongside relaxation. Shore excursions are equally impressive, such as private tours of the Scottish Highlands or exclusive access to the opera houses of Vienna. These experiences align your brand with sophistication, heritage, and global perspective.

Photo Courtesy of Cunard

WHY IMMERSIVE EXPERIENCES MATTER

Immersive experiences allow brands to break through the noise and create emotional connections with their audiences. They transform events from transactional interactions into meaningful stories that participants will associate with the brand for years to come. By leveraging the unique settings and exceptional service of cruise lines, brands can craft moments that are unforgettable, impactful, and deeply resonant.

Whether it's the ultra-luxury of Regent Seven Seas, the adventurous energy of Norwegian Cruise Line, or the timeless elegance of Cunard, cruise experiences provide the ideal platform for creating lasting brand memories. These immersive events engage the senses, spark emotion, and reinforce the values and vision of your brand in ways no traditional venue can match.

Turning Experiences Into Legacies

To create a truly impactful event, brands must focus on designing experiences that reflect their identity while resonating with their audience's desires. Immersive moments on cruise lines provide the perfect opportunity to foster connection, loyalty, and admiration. By combining stunning destinations, tailored activities, and impeccable service, these experiences ensure your brand is remembered and cherished.

For those ready to elevate their branding strategy, the power of immersive experiences awaits. Whether it's through cultural discovery, adrenaline-pumping adventure, or serene luxury, these moments create stories that attendees will carry with them forever. The journey begins here, where your brand's legacy takes shape on the open seas.

Events Are the Place for Discovering Products, People, and News

Events are the ultimate platform for discovering new products and announcements, offering a dynamic environment where brands can showcase their latest innovations and share exciting news directly with their audience. The interactive nature of events allows attendees to experience products firsthand through live demonstrations, creating a memorable and impactful introduction. Product demos at events provide an invaluable opportunity to highlight the unique features and benefits of your offerings. By allowing attendees to see, touch, and test products in real time, you can create a deeper connection and understanding that static presentations or online content simply can't match. Engaging demonstrations can capture the attention of your audience, demonstrate practical applications, and address questions on the spot.

In addition to product demos, events are a prime venue for making significant announcements and sharing news. Whether you are launching a new product, unveiling a strategic partnership, or announcing company milestones, doing so at an event ensures your message reaches a highly engaged and relevant audience. The buzz and excitement generated by live announcements can amplify the impact of your news, creating a sense of exclusivity and immediacy. To maximize the reach of your announcements, leverage the power of social media and live streaming. Broadcasting your announcements in real-time on event pages allows you to extend the excitement to a broader audience who may not be able to attend in person. This approach not only increases visibility but also fosters a sense of inclusion and community among your followers.

Moreover, events provide a unique opportunity for face-to-face interaction with key stakeholders, including customers, partners, and media representatives. This personal engagement allows for immediate feedback, creating a two-way dialogue that can provide valuable insights and strengthen relationships. Hosting Q&A sessions, panel discussions, and meet-and-greet opportunities further enhances the interactive experience, ensuring your audience feels valued and heard.

5

ALIGNING EVENT BRANDING WITH OVERALL BRAND STRATEGY

Aligning event branding with your overall brand strategy ensures consistency and enhances the impact of your brand across all touchpoints. Focusing on identity and messaging and allowing the event to stand out as its own brand are key aspects of this alignment.

REFLECT YOUR IDENTITY

The visual identity of your event should mirror your overall brand while creating a unique and memorable experience. Start by incorporating your brand's logo, color schemes, and typography into all event materials, including invitations, name badges, digital assets, and merchandise. Consistency in these visual elements reinforces your brand identity and ensures recognition. However, your event can also have its own distinct visual style that complements your brand. This might include specific themes or design elements unique to the event but still aligned with your brand's aesthetic.

BE TRUE TO YOUR MESSAGING AND COMMUNICATION STRATEGY

Consistency in messaging and communication is crucial for reinforcing your brand's values and narrative. All event communications, from promotional materials to on-site announcements, should reflect your brand's tone of voice. Develop key messages that align with your brand's overall strategy and ensure they are conveyed through speeches, presentations, social media posts, and other communications. Tailor your messaging to the specific audience and objectives of the event while maintaining alignment with your brand's core messages. Effective storytelling that integrates your brand's mission and values creates a compelling and cohesive experience for attendees.

EVENTS CAN BE THEIR OWN BRANDS

While alignment with your overall brand strategy is important, events can also stand out as distinct brands. Create a unique identity and experience that is memorable and engaging. Develop a specific theme or concept for your event that differentiates it from other brand activities and makes it a special occasion. This could include unique branding elements such as event slogans, custom graphics, and exclusive merchandise.

By doing so, your event becomes an extension of your brand with its own personality and appeal. This dual approach ensures the event reflects your brand while offering a distinctive experience that resonates with attendees.

EVENTS = SOCIAL MEDIA PARADISE FOR BRANDS

Events present a unique opportunity to amplify your brand's presence on social media, creating a vibrant and interactive digital environment that extends beyond the physical venue. With the right strategy, you can transform your event into a social media paradise, generating buzz, engagement, and lasting impressions.

REAL-TIME ENGAGEMENT

Events provide a wealth of real-time content that can be shared across social media platforms. Live updates, behind-the-scenes glimpses, and instant reactions from attendees create a dynamic stream of content that captures the excitement and energy of the event. Utilizing event-specific hashtags helps consolidate these posts, making it easier for participants to follow and join the conversation.

USER-GENERATED CONTENT

Encouraging attendees to share their experiences on social media is a powerful way to generate authentic, user-generated content. Set up photo booths, branded backdrops, and interactive installations that are visually appealing and encourage attendees to take and share photos. Running contests or giveaways that reward social media posts can further incentivize sharing, increasing your event's reach and visibility.

INFLUENCER COLLABORATION

Partnering with influencers and industry leaders to attend and promote your event can significantly boost your social media presence. Influencers bring their own following to the event, expanding your reach and lending credibility to your brand. Encourage them to share their experiences, tag your brand, and use the event hashtag to maximize impact.

POST-EVENT CONTENT BANK

After the event, share highlights and key moments on your social media channels. Posting recaps, video montages, and standout quotes or images helps sustain the event's momentum and keeps your brand top-of-mind. Encourage attendees to share their own highlights and testimonials, further extending the event's social media life.

FOLLOW-UP IS KEY FOR EVENTS

Following up after an event is crucial for maximizing its impact and ensuring continuous improvement. Effective follow-up strategies include collecting feedback through surveys, analyzing participant experiences, monitoring relevant KPIs, utilizing data, and assessing revenue outcomes. These actions provide valuable insights, strengthen attendee relationships, and enhance future events.

CONDUCT SURVEYS

Surveys are essential for gathering attendee feedback. Send out well-designed, branded surveys shortly after the event to capture fresh and accurate responses. Include questions about various aspects such as presentation quality, content relevance, networking opportunities, and overall satisfaction. Open questions offer deeper insights and suggestions for improvement. Analyzing survey results helps understand what worked well and areas needing enhancement, ensuring future events better meet attendee expectations.

LEVERAGE DATA

Utilize data collected before, during, and after the event for continuous improvement and personalization. Analyze attendee demographics, behavioral data, and feedback to identify trends and preferences. This informs content selection, speaker choices, marketing strategies, and personalized communications, tailoring events to audience needs and enhancing satisfaction.

MONITOR KPIS

Track Key Performance Indicators (KPIs) to quantitatively measure event success. Monitor attendance rates, participant engagement (e.g., session participation, app usage, social media interactions), lead generation, conversion rates, and overall satisfaction ratings. Analyzing these metrics provides insights into event effectiveness and alignment with strategic objectives, guiding decisions for future improvements.

What to Communicate after the Event

Beyond surveys and data analysis aligned with your KPIs, effective communication can extend the event's impact long after it concludes. Brands that plan post-event communication are more likely to enhance attendee experiences and generate interest from those who did not attend.

Follow-up & Thank You

Send thank-you emails to attendees and encourage them to participate in your short survey. Provide access to event recordings, presentations, and other valuable materials. This gesture shows appreciation and extends the event's value beyond its duration.

Post-Event Content

Utilize social media and your website to share event content such as photos, videos, and testimonials. This content reinforces key moments and engages both attendees and a broader audience.

RETENTION

Convert event participants into newsletter sub-scribers. Send a sequence of relevant emails, including thank-you notes, access to recordings, special offers, and early event sign-up opportunities for your future events. Cultivating this relationship fosters loyalty and encourages repeat attendance. After the event is a perfect opportunity to build that desirable community that we have talked about. Let the attendees interact with each other so they can feel attached to your brand and like-minded people.

6

THE NEW HORIZON: LEVERAGING TECHNOLOGY AND AI FOR NEXT-LEVEL EVENT BRANDING

The landscape of branding and events is evolving at an unprecedented pace, largely due to advancements in technology and artificial intelligence (AI). These tools are no longer merely "nice-to-haves"; they are becoming essential drivers of effective, immersive, and memorable brand experiences. In this chapter, we delve into the transformative role of technology and AI in event branding, exploring how they enhance engagement, streamline personalization, and amplify impact. As we look forward, it's clear that embracing technology and AI will shape the future of brand events, allowing companies to connect with audiences in powerful new ways.

THE ROLE OF TECHNOLOGY IN MODERN EVENT BRANDING

Technology has already reshaped how brands interact with audiences. At events, it serves as both a vehicle for engagement and a bridge between the brand and its attendees. As brands compete for attention, the goal is to create interactive experiences that captivate, inform, and resonate with audiences. Technology enables brands to bring these elements to life, enhancing every aspect of the event, from planning and logistics to the experience itself.

Some of the most impactful technologies used in event branding include augmented reality (AR), virtual reality (VR), mobile apps, live streaming, and interactive displays. Each of these tools offers unique opportunities for brands to create a cohesive experience that aligns with their message and values, allowing attendees to engage in meaningful ways.

Cruise ships are continually enhancing their connectivity, and one of the most significant advancements in recent years has been the integration of SpaceX's Starlink satellite internet onboard. With cutting-edge technology, Starlink delivers robust internet capabilities that keep passengers and conference attendees seamlessly connected at sea. According to Starlink's specifications, download speeds range from 40 Mbps to over 200 Mbps, while upload speeds reach 8 to more than 25 Mbps, all with latency under 99 milliseconds. This reliable, high-speed connectivity ensures cruise ships can support everything from real-time video conferencing to streaming and interactive digital experiences, making them an increasingly viable option for modern corporate events and conferences. To mitigate potential disruptions, we recommend saving all presentations on a USB drive as a backup in case of Wi-Fi issues during the conference.

Each of these tools offers unique opportunities for brands to create a cohesive experience that aligns with their message and values, allowing attendees to engage in meaningful ways.

For example, AR and VR can be used to create immersive product demonstrations, allowing attendees to experience a brand's offerings as if they were interacting with them in the real world. Mobile apps, meanwhile, offer an efficient way to provide event information, agendas, and personalized recommendations, making the event experience seamless and enjoyable for attendees.

AI AND THE FUTURE OF PERSONALIZATION

Artificial intelligence is redefining personalization in ways that were previously unimaginable. AI allows for a deeper understanding of each attendee for branded events, enabling companies to create hyper-personalized experiences. Through AI, brands can gather and analyze attendee data such as past interactions, preferences, and engagement patterns before, during, and after the event. This insight allows brands to craft tailored content, suggest relevant sessions, and provide individualized interactions that make attendees feel valued and understood.

Imagine attending a conference where every session, product demonstration, or networking opportunity is suggested based on your interests and past engagements with the brand. AI enables this level of customization, creating a journey that resonates with each individual. This personalized experience enhances engagement and strengthens the emotional connection between the attendee and the brand.

KEY WAYS TECHNOLOGY AND AI ENHANCE BRANDING THROUGH EVENTS

1. Creating Immersive Experiences

With AR and VR, brands can create multi-sensory experiences that transport attendees into a different environment, allowing them to interact with the brand in a memorable way. Imagine a travel brand using VR to give attendees a virtual tour of its top destinations or an automotive company using AR to let attendees explore the interior of a new car model. These technologies create a hands-on experience that connects attendees to the brand's offerings on a deeper level.

2. Enhanced Engagement Through Gamification

Gamification, powered by AI and digital platforms, has become popular for driving event engagement. By introducing game-like elements such as points, leaderboards, and rewards, brands can encourage attendees to participate in sessions actively, interact with exhibits, or network with other attendees. AI-driven gamification allows brands to personalize challenges and rewards based on attendee behavior, making the experience fun and relevant.

For instance, a technology company might create a scavenger hunt within the event, encouraging attendees to explore different booths and interact with brand representatives. As attendees collect points or earn prizes, they become more engaged with the brand and develop positive associations with the experience.

3. AI-Driven Personalization

AI's ability to process vast amounts of data in real time enables brands to offer unique, personalized experiences to each attendee. From suggesting sessions that align with their interests to tailoring networking recommendations, AI creates a highly customized event experience. This personalization deepens brand loyalty by making attendees feel seen and understood.

Consider an event app that uses AI to recommend sessions, exhibitors, and networking opportunities based on an attendee's profile. This app might remind a healthcare professional of sessions focused on new medical technologies or direct a marketing executive to workshops on AI in advertising. By curating an agenda that reflects individual interests, the brand ensures a more meaningful and memorable experience.

4. Improving Real-Time Engagement and Feedback

Real-time feedback tools powered by AI allow brands to gauge attendee sentiment and engagement instantly. During sessions, AI can analyze reactions, monitor engagement levels, and even adapt content to maintain interest. This immediate feedback enables brands to make on-the-spot adjustments, ensuring a more dynamic and responsive experience.

For instance, AI-driven sentiment analysis tools can detect if attendees are losing interest or becoming highly engaged with specific content. Event organizers can then adjust the session's format or pace to keep the audience engaged. This adaptability demonstrates the brand's commitment to attendee satisfaction, creating a positive impression that resonates long after the event.

5. Streamlining Logistics and Enhancing Efficiency

AI and technology also streamline event logistics, making it easier to plan and execute complex events seamlessly. Chatbots powered by AI can handle common attendee questions, mobile apps provide on-demand access to schedules, and automated registration systems reduce wait times and minimize errors.

Consider an event with thousands of attendees. An AI-powered chatbot can handle registration inquiries, provide event information, and offer personalized recommendations based on individual preferences. This automation allows event staff to focus on creating engaging experiences rather than handling logistical issues, ensuring a smooth, enjoyable event for everyone.

6. Extending Reach Through Live Streaming and Hybrid Events

With live streaming and hybrid event capabilities, brands can extend their reach beyond physical attendees. Streaming sessions or keynotes allows remote attendees to experience the event in real time, and interactive features such as live chat and Q&A sessions enable them to participate actively. This increased accessibility allows brands to reach a global audience, building a broader base of engaged followers.

Imagine a fashion brand launching a new line at a live event. By live-streaming the launch to social media, the brand reaches a much larger audience, creating excitement and engagement even among those who couldn't attend in person. Hybrid events bridge the gap between physical and digital experiences, broadening the brand's reach and influence.

THE LONG-TERM BENEFITS OF TECH-ENHANCED EVENT BRANDING

BUILDING LASTING CONNECTIONS

Technology allows brands to create lasting connections by crafting experiences that resonate on a personal level. Attendees who feel engaged and valued are more likely to become brand advocates, sharing their positive experiences with friends, family, and followers. By using technology to foster these connections, brands can transform event attendees into loyal customers and enthusiastic promoters.

KEITH LEFKOF, ECC, TAE

MEASURABLE INSIGHTS AND DATA-DRIVEN STRATEGIES

The data collected through AI and digital tools provides valuable insights into attendee behavior, preferences, and engagement patterns. Brands can use this data to refine their event strategies, ensuring future events are even more impactful and aligned with audience needs. With AI, brands can make informed decisions that enhance their branding efforts, increasing return on investment and improving overall effectiveness.

ELEVATING BRAND PERCEPTION THROUGH INNOVATION

Events that incorporate cutting-edge technology and AI demonstrate a brand's commitment to innovation. This association elevates brand perception, positioning the company as forward-thinking and adaptable. Attendees are likely to associate the brand with creativity, intelligence, and progress, making a positive impression that extends well beyond the event itself.

THE FUTURE OF AI AND TECHNOLOGY IN EVENT BRANDING

The future of branding through events will be marked by ever-evolving technological advancements. As AI continues to develop, brands will be able to offer even more personalized, immersive experiences that captivate and inspire. We can expect the following trends to shape the future:

1. **Hyper-Personalization**: AI will continue to refine personalization, creating highly customized event experiences for each attendee.
2. **Augmented and Mixed Reality**: AR and MR will become more widely accessible, enabling brands to create multi-dimensional experiences that blur the lines between digital and physical realms.
3. **Predictive Analytics**: With AI-driven predictive analytics, brands will be able to anticipate attendee preferences and engagement levels, tailoring content in advance.
4. **Automation in Real-Time Adaptation**: As AI gains the ability to adapt content in real time, event experiences will become even more dynamic and responsive to audience needs.
5. **Sustainable Tech-Enhanced Events**: As sustainability becomes a priority, tech solutions will make event branding eco-friendly, reducing waste and environmental impact.

THE TECH-POWERED PATH TO BRAND SUCCESS

The integration of technology and AI into event branding is a game-changer, enabling brands to create immersive, personalized, and engaging experiences that drive meaningful connections. These tools not only elevate the quality and impact of branded events but also position the brand as innovative and forward-thinking, attributes that resonate with modern consumers. By embracing technology and AI, companies can deliver memorable events that amplify their brand's reach and reinforce its message, paving the way for sustainable growth and long-term success.

In a world where experiences are the new currency, tech-enhanced event branding offers brands a powerful opportunity to connect, inspire, and stand out. The future of branding is here, and it's as engaging, immersive, and impactful as technology can make it.

LEVERAGING EVENT TECHNOLOGY - PROJECTION MAPPING

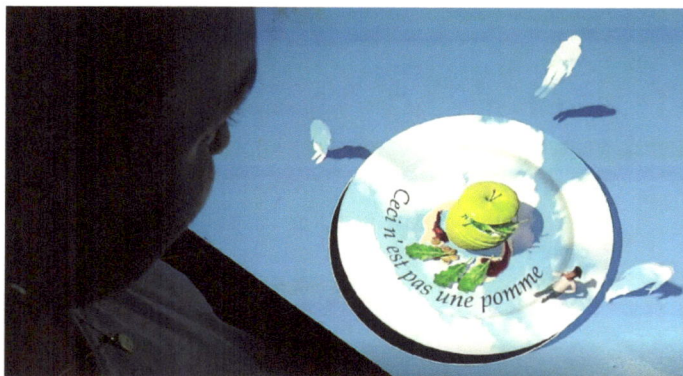

Photo Courtesy of Celebrity Cruises

Pictures Courtesy of Celebrity Cruises

Celebrity Cruises has revolutionized the guest experience with its innovative use of projection mapping, turning ordinary moments into extraordinary, immersive memories that linger long after the journey ends. At the forefront of this innovation is the *Le Petit Chef* dining experience, a captivating blend of technology, storytelling, and culinary artistry. Guests are treated to a unique spectacle as a tiny, animated chef comes to life on their table, preparing each dish with charm and whimsy through 3D projection mapping. As the virtual chef performs, the real-life dish is served in perfect harmony, creating a seamless fusion of entertainment and gastronomy that elevates dining to an unforgettable event.

This seamless fusion of technology and gastronomy is an interactive branding experience that embodies Celebrity Cruises' luxury and innovation. By transforming dining tables into interactive spaces, Le Petit Chef highlights the cruise line's dedication to delivering extraordinary, tech-driven experiences. The projection mapping brings the brand's values of creativity and modern luxury to life, making the meal not just a sensory delight but also a memorable brand interaction.

The initiative has played a pivotal role in positioning ships like the Celebrity Edge as leaders in innovation within the cruise industry. By enhancing guest engagement and sparking social media buzz, this technology-driven experience amplifies brand visibility in a dynamic, versatile manner. It aligns perfectly with Celebrity's brand messaging, creating real-time, immersive interactions that resonate with passengers long after they leave the ship.

The brilliance of the Le Petit Chef dining experience lies not only in its theatrical presentation but also in its ability to draw guests into the brand story of Celebrity Cruises. As the tiny chef playfully prepares meals on the table, the underlying message of innovation and modern luxury resonates. Each meal, crafted with precision, reflects the same attention to detail that Celebrity Cruises pours into every aspect of its brand experience. The 3D projection mapping serves as a canvas for storytelling, aligning the chef's culinary journey with Celebrity's own journey of excellence and forward-thinking guest service.

This sophisticated use of projection mapping is a strategic move for the cruise line. By intertwining entertainment, technology, and brand narrative, Le Petit Chef enhances brand engagement in an organic, memorable way. Guests leave with a heightened awareness of the brand's commitment to quality and innovation, making them more likely to share their experiences on social media or recommend the cruise to others.

The integration of Le Petit Chef reinforces Celebrity Cruises' positioning as a leader in the luxury cruise market. Tapping into the emotional responses of guests' surprise, delight, and curiosity fosters a deeper connection with the brand. The immersive, dynamic nature of projection mapping creates a touchpoint that differentiates Celebrity from other cruise lines, making it clear that innovation and guest satisfaction are at the heart of the brand's ethos.

Moreover, this branding experience shows the versatility of projection mapping beyond mere entertainment. By transforming an ordinary dinner into a branded spectacle, Celebrity Cruises demonstrates how technology can be harnessed to reinforce brand identity while simultaneously elevating the customer experience. This dynamic branding approach ensures that guests associate Celebrity Cruises with cutting-edge luxury, creating lasting impressions and positive word-of-mouth that extend far beyond the ship.

In summary, Le Petit Chef's use of 3D projection mapping not only enhances the onboard experience but serves as a powerful branding tool. It showcases the brand's values of innovation and luxury, driving home the message that Celebrity Cruises is at the forefront of technological and guest experience advancements. This approach provides an exciting model for how brands can leverage projection mapping to create memorable, engaging, and brand-aligned experiences in a competitive industry.

HERE'S HOW THIS CAN BE ACHIEVED:

1. Custom Branded Animations

- **Personalize the Chef's Story**: Customize the animation to reflect the brand's story. For example, if the event is for a luxury brand, the chef's narrative can be themed around elegance, craftsmanship, and quality, mirroring the values of the brand. The animation could depict the brand's journey, products, or history playfully and engagingly.

- **Incorporate Brand Elements**: The visuals can include the brand's logo, color schemes, and messaging throughout the dining experience. Each course prepared by Le Petit Chef can align with a specific product or aspect of the brand, turning each meal into a marketing touchpoint.

2. Product Launch or Showcase

- **Themed Dishes Around Products**: If the event is for a product launch, the dishes presented by Le Petit Chef can symbolically represent the features of the new product. For instance, a tech company could use the animations to showcase product innovation by having the animated chef "assemble" a device piece by piece as part of the meal preparation, making the dining experience a metaphor for the product's creation process.

- **Interactive Voting or Engagement**: Like in the "Le Petit Chef and Friends" version, the audience can be invited to vote on a favorite dish, each dish representing a different product or service. This not only involves guests interactively but also creates a competitive aspect, enhancing brand engagement.

3. Storytelling Aligned with Brand Values

- **Brand's Heritage and Values**: For events focusing on a brand's legacy, Le Petit Chef can take guests through a culinary journey that tells the brand's history, innovation milestones, or global presence. The chef could traverse different landscapes and eras tied to the brand's evolution, using humor and creativity to reinforce key messages.
- **Cultural or Themed Branding**: For brands associated with particular regions or cultural experiences, the animation could adapt to present cultural dishes that tie into the brand's identity (e.g., Italian for a fashion brand from Italy). This approach deepens the guests' connection to the brand.

4. Creating a Social Media Buzz

- **Shareable Moments**: The animated, interactive dining experience creates memorable and shareable moments. Encourage guests to capture videos and photos of the projection mapping and share them on social media, using branded hashtags or event-specific promotions. This spreads the brand's message organically and enhances digital visibility.

5. Luxury and Exclusive Experience

- **VIP and Exclusive Events**: Position Le Petit Chef as part of an exclusive experience for high-profile clients or VIPs. This luxury dining encounter aligns with high-end brands and events, offering not just a meal but an artistic, immersive experience that guests associate with sophistication and exclusivity.

7

CHARTING THE COURSE FOR SUCCESS: MASTERING THE INTRICACIES OF CRUISE EVENT PLANNING

Planning a corporate conference aboard a cruise ship is both an exhilarating and complex endeavor, requiring meticulous attention to detail, advanced coordination, and an understanding of how to seamlessly orchestrate an event in a dynamic, floating environment. In this crucial chapter, we introduce the essential steps needed to make a corporate cruise conference a resounding success. With the venue constantly on the move and ever-changing backdrops, proper planning and expertise are vital. This chapter explores the importance of a strategic approach and the value of working with an experienced travel advisor to achieve seamless, flawless execution.

The journey begins with thoroughly reviewing the corporation's conference goals, vision, and budget.

Understanding these elements is essential as they guide every subsequent decision. The goals typically encompass professional development, team building, and networking opportunities, while the vision might include a mix of formal sessions and informal interactions in an inspiring environment. Budget considerations are crucial, as they dictate the scope and scale of the event.

One of the first steps in the planning process is selecting the right cruise line and itinerary. This decision is crucial as it sets the stage for the entire event. A travel advisor with specialized knowledge in cruise conferences can be your guiding star, providing invaluable insights and helping you choose the best options that align with your conference objectives.

Next, developing a detailed schedule is vital. This schedule should balance professional activities, such as keynote speeches and breakout sessions, with leisure and team-building opportunities. A cruise's unique setting allows for creative planning, including sessions on deck, networking events under the stars, and excursions at various destinations that can double as team-building activities.

Budget management is another critical component. A comprehensive budget should account for all aspects, including cruise booking, accommodation, meals, activities, and contingency funds. Working with a travel advisor can help identify cost-saving opportunities, such as group rates and all-inclusive packages, ensuring the budget is optimized without compromising quality.

Logistical considerations include arranging advanced audiovisual equipment, ensuring reliable internet access, and coordinating personalized conference materials. Developing contingency plans for potential disruptions, such as weather-related issues, is essential to maintain the conference schedule.

Effective communication and coordination are pivotal throughout the planning process. Regular updates and adjustments ensure that all details are covered and that the conference goals and vision are consistently aligned with the progress of the planning.

By following a proven process and leveraging the expertise of a travel advisor, the intricacies of cruise conference logistics can be navigated successfully. This approach not only ensures a smooth and well-organized event but also enhances the overall experience, making the cruise conference a memorable and impactful journey for all participants.

A successful cruise conference also hinges on effectively integrating various elements to create a cohesive and engaging event.

Venue Selection and Customization: It is vital to choose the right cruise ship that can be tailored to meet the conference's specific needs. The ship should offer versatile meeting spaces that can be customized for various activities, from large keynote sessions to intimate breakout discussions. Ensuring these venues are equipped with the latest technology and comfortable furnishings will contribute to the event's overall success.

Onboard Activities and Excursions: A cruise conference's unique aspect is its ability to blend professional development with leisure and adventure. Organizers should carefully select and schedule onboard activities and shore excursions that complement the conference goals. Activities such as guided tours, snorkeling, cultural visits, and adventure sports can be excellent team-building exercises and provide memorable experiences that strengthen professional relationships. This shared experience of adventure and learning can foster a sense of unity and engagement among the conference participants.

Catering and Hospitality: High-quality catering and hospitality services are essential to maintaining attendee satisfaction. Cruise ships often offer diverse dining options and customizable menus that can accommodate various dietary needs and preferences. Ensuring a seamless dining experience, from casual meals to formal gala dinners, enhances the overall attendee experience.

Branding and Personalization: Infusing the corporate brand into the cruise experience helps reinforce the company's identity and message. This can be achieved through customized signage, branded materials, and tailored events that reflect the company's culture and values. Personalized touches, such as welcome kits, branded merchandise, and tailored communication, can make attendees feel valued and connected to the Event.

Health and Safety: Ensuring the health and safety of all participants is paramount. This includes implementing stringent health protocols and emergency preparedness plans and providing accessible medical facilities onboard. Clear communication about health and safety measures reassures attendees and contributes to a stress-free conference experience.

After the Event, remember to conduct a thorough post-event evaluation. This step is not just a formality but a crucial part of the planning process. By gathering feedback from attendees and analyzing the Event's success, you can identify areas for improvement and refine your planning process. This continuous improvement cycle is the key to ensuring that your future conferences are even more successful.

The logistics of organizing a cruise conference are complex but manageable with proper planning and expertise. By focusing on detailed preparation, leveraging the knowledge of travel advisors, and aligning with the company's goals and vision, a cruise conference can transcend the traditional event experience. It becomes a dynamic and engaging journey that fosters professional growth, enhances team cohesion, and leaves a lasting impact on every participant. This chapter provides a comprehensive guide to mastering the intricacies of cruise conference logistics, paving the way for innovative and unforgettable corporate events on the high seas.

GOALS: DEFINING THE PURPOSE AND OBJECTIVES

The foundation of any successful corporate cruise conference lies in clearly defined goals. Understanding the purpose and objectives of the event is essential as it guides every aspect of planning and execution. When Inc. Air Trampoline Park. set out to host their annual conference aboard the Utopia of the Seas, its goals were multifaceted: fostering innovation, enhancing team cohesion, and celebrating the year's achievements.

By setting these goals, the company could craft a focused agenda that aligned with its strategic objectives. Keynote speeches by industry leaders, interactive workshops, and team-building excursions were meticulously planned to inspire the attendees' creativity, collaboration, and celebration. Without clear goals, the conference could have quickly devolved into disjointed activities, failing to deliver the desired impact.

VISION: CREATING A MEMORABLE EXPERIENCE

The vision for a corporate cruise conference goes beyond just the goals; it's about creating a memorable experience that resonates with attendees long after the ship docks. For Big Air Trampoline Park, their vision for their franchisees was to blend professional development with celebrating their success while providing an unforgettable immersive experience through the Caribbean's stunning journey. This vision shaped every decision, from the selection of the cruise itinerary to the design of the conference's branding and thematic elements.

Imagine the powerful impact of hosting a keynote session in a conference room with panoramic ocean views or organizing team-building activities that include snorkeling in crystal-clear waters or exploring ancient ruins. These unique experiences create a sense of adventure and camaraderie and foster a deep sense of unity and engagement among the attendees, making the conference not just a professional obligation but an exciting journey that attendees eagerly anticipate.

BUDGET CONSIDERATIONS: BALANCING COST AND QUALITY

Budget considerations are paramount in planning any corporate event, and a cruise conference is no exception. A well-defined budget ensures the event is financially viable while delivering a high-quality experience. For the Big Air Trampoline Park franchise, this meant carefully allocating resources to cover various expenses, from cruise bookings and accommodations to meals, activities, and contingencies.

Working with an experienced travel advisor was crucial in this regard. The advisor helped the company secure group rates, take advantage of all-inclusive packages, and identify cost-saving opportunities without compromising on quality. This included negotiating better deals for conference facilities, AV equipment, and onboard activities. By meticulously tracking expenses and staying within the budget, the company could maximize the return on investment and ensure financial prudence.

THE IMPORTANCE OF PROFESSIONAL GUIDANCE IN CRUISE CONFERENCE PLANNING CUSTOMIZABLE PACKAGES AND COST EFFICIENCY

One significant advantage of hosting a conference on a cruise ship is the availability of customizable packages. Cruise lines offer all-inclusive options that bundle accommodation, meals, meeting spaces, and entertainment into one package. This approach not only simplifies budgeting but also provides cost efficiency. By choosing the right package, companies can manage costs more effectively and avoid unexpected expenses.

LEVERAGING TECHNOLOGY FOR BUDGET MANAGEMENT

Technology plays a crucial role in budget management. Tools provided by platforms like CruiseTech IQ, which you will learn more about throughout this book, allow organizers to monitor and adjust the budget in real time. These tools facilitate detailed tracking of all expenses, from initial deposits to final payments, ensuring transparency and control over financial resources. Real-time budget tracking also helps make informed decisions and adjustments on the fly, preventing overspending and ensuring that all financial goals are met.

In the fast-paced world of corporate event planning, CruiseTech IQ stands out with its distinctive project and event management solutions, tailor-made for cruise conferences. Picture a voyage where your corporate event is transformed into an extraordinary experience on a luxurious cruise ship. Their innovative platform, powered by the renowned Trippus event management system with a wealth of 25 years of industry experience, is the ultimate Cruise Conference Planning Command Center, offering unparalleled features and advantages.

From initial concept to post-event evaluation, CruiseTech IQ stands by your side, providing the expertise and technology needed to transform your corporate vision into a remarkable reality. By embracing the unique advantages of a cruise setting and leveraging our platform, your next corporate conference can achieve unprecedented success, leaving a lasting impression on all who attend. Imagine a corporate event transcending the ordinary, becoming a journey of innovation, engagement, and inspiration.

INTEGRATING GOALS, VISION, AND BUDGET: THE KEY TO SUCCESSFUL CRUISE CONFERENCE EXECUTION

By clearly defining the goals, the company was able to prioritize activities and allocate resources accordingly. The vision provided a guiding light for all creative and logistical decisions, ensuring that the conference was not just productive but also memorable and inspiring. The budget acted as a practical framework, ensuring that all plans were financially sustainable. The successful alignment of these three elements brought a sense of accomplishment and empowerment to the team.

The Crucial Role of a Skilled Travel Professional or Meeting Planner

Planning a successful cruise conference is a multi-faceted endeavor that demands meticulous attention to logistics, itineraries, and budgets challenges that can overwhelm even seasoned corporate teams. This is where the expertise of a skilled travel professional or meeting planner, particularly one specializing in corporate events, becomes not just helpful but essential. While many travel advisors excel in arranging luxury family vacations or bucket-list safaris, orchestrating a large-scale corporate event requires a distinct skill set. Choosing the wrong advisor can lead to logistical chaos, unmet goals, and a tarnished reputation, turning what should be a dream conference into a nightmare.

A true corporate event planning expert brings a strategic vision to every aspect of the event. They understand the intricacies of coordinating multiple stakeholders, balancing budgets, and creating a seamless and engaging conference experience. Their ability to align the client's goals and aspirations with the attendee experience sets them apart. From crafting tailored itineraries to managing vendor negotiations, these professionals ensure every detail is handled with precision, resulting in a polished and impactful event.

Far more than just organizers, skilled planners act as strategic partners, integrating their industry expertise and practical experience to streamline the planning process. They serve as an extension of the corporate team, offering tailored recommendations for cruise lines, venues, and activities that align with the event's vision and objectives. Acting as a single point of contact, they manage the intricate web of communication between all the stakeholders, the clients, attendees, cruise lines, vendors, and service providers, ensuring a collaborative and efficient approach that leaves no detail overlooked.

The complexities of cruise conference planning demand a holistic approach that aligns goals, vision, and budget into a cohesive strategy. A skilled travel professional transforms this complexity into a seamless process, designing an experience that captivates attendees and achieves organizational objectives. Their role is critical not only in logistical execution but also in ensuring the event fosters team cohesion, supports strategic aims, and creates lasting memories for all participants.

For organizations seeking to elevate their corporate cruise conferences to extraordinary levels, the key lies in combining the expertise of an experienced planner with advanced event management tools like CruiseTech IQ. This comprehensive approach ensures that every phase of the event from concept to execution to post-event evaluation is handled with care and precision.

The result is a resounding success: a truly unforgettable event that exceeds expectations, achieves strategic goals, and strengthens the brand's reputation. With the guidance of a skilled travel professional or meeting planner, companies can confidently transform their vision into a reality that resonates far beyond the event itself.

Pre-Process Planning and On-Board Communication

In the fast-paced world of corporate event planning, CruiseTech IQ stands out with its distinctive project and event management solutions, tailor-made for cruise conferences. Picture a voyage where your corporate event is transformed into an extraordinary experience on a luxurious cruise ship. Our innovative platform, powered by the renowned Trippus event management system with a wealth of 25 years of industry experience, is the ultimate Cruise Conference Planning Command Center, offering unparalleled features and advantages.

Envision the excitement and anticipation as your team embarks on an extraordinary sea journey. The process begins with a meticulous examination of your corporation's conference objectives, vision, and budget. These elements serve as the guiding principles for every subsequent decision, from selecting the ideal cruise line and itinerary to crafting a comprehensive schedule that harmonizes professional activities with leisure and team-building opportunities. This rigorous planning ensures that every aspect of your cruise conference is meticulously planned and executed, leaving no room for unexpected surprises.

CruiseTech IQ tackles the unique challenges of organizing events on cruise ships with a comprehensive suite of tools designed to ensure seamless integration, stakeholder collaboration, and unparalleled attendee experiences. Envision a custom-branded website that simplifies registration, mobile apps that personalize attendee engagement, and real-time adjustments to schedules and logistics. These tools facilitate effective communication, robust task management, and efficient resource allocation, ensuring every conference runs smoothly with minimal disruptions.

Envision your attendees accessing personalized agendas through mobile apps, receiving real-time notifications about session changes, and engaging digitally with other participants and speakers. This level of engagement enhances their experience and fosters deeper involvement with the conference's offerings. Real-time coordination tools provided by CruiseTech IQ prove indispensable, allowing for swift modifications in response to unexpected changes such as weather conditions or technical difficulties, thus maintaining a professional and enjoyable atmosphere throughout the event.

Meticulous planning extends to catering and hospitality services, ensuring high-quality dining experiences that cater to various dietary needs and preferences. Diverse dining options and customizable menus enhance the overall attendee experience, making every meal a memorable part of the conference. Branding and personalization are also crucial, with customized signage, branded materials, and tailored events that reflect the company's culture and values. Personalized touches like welcome kits and branded merchandise make attendees feel valued and connected to the event.

After the event, conducting a thorough post-event evaluation is crucial for understanding the conference's success and identifying areas for improvement. Gathering feedback through surveys and discussions provides valuable insights into what worked well and what could be enhanced for future events, ensuring a continuous improvement cycle.

THE IMPORTANCE OF TRAVEL INSURANCE FOR CRUISE CONFERENCE ATTENDEES

When planning a corporate cruise conference, ensuring the safety and well-being of all attendees is paramount. One critical aspect often overlooked is the importance of travel insurance. Travel insurance provides a safety net that can protect against unforeseen events, offering a sense of security and relief. Utilizing information from Allianz Travel Insurance, we can fully understand why this coverage is indispensable for cruise and travel participants.

COMPREHENSIVE COVERAGE FOR UNFORESEEN EVENTS

Travel insurance offers comprehensive coverage that protects attendees against various unexpected incidents. These can include trip cancellations, interruptions, delays, lost or delayed baggage, medical emergencies, and more. Given the complexities of travel and the unique environment of a cruise ship, such coverage is crucial.

TRIP CANCELLATION AND INTERRUPTION

Corporate events involve significant investments in terms of time and money. Travel insurance can reimburse the non-refundable expenses if an attendee has to cancel their trip due to a covered reason, such as illness, injury, or unforeseen work obligations. Similarly, if the trip is interrupted say, if an attendee needs to return home early due to a family emergency travel insurance can cover the additional costs incurred for the return journey and any prepaid expenses for the missed portion of the trip.

TRAVEL DELAYS

Travel delays are expected due to weather, mechanical issues, or other unforeseen circumstances. Travel insurance can reimburse expenses such as hotel stays, meals, and transportation for covered travel delays, ensuring attendees are not out-of-pocket for these unexpected costs.

LOST OR DELAYED BAGGAGE

Luggage can sometimes be lost, stolen, or delayed. Travel insurance covers replacing essential items and clothing, ensuring attendees can continue their conference activities without significant disruptions. This is particularly important for a cruise, where retrieving lost baggage can be more complicated than on land.

MEDICAL EMERGENCIES

Medical emergencies can occur at any time, and being on a cruise ship presents unique challenges for medical care. Allianz Travel Insurance covers medical expenses if an attendee becomes ill or injured during the trip. This can include hospital stays, doctor visits, and medications. Importantly, it also covers medical evacuation, which can be incredibly costly but necessary if an attendee needs to be transported to the nearest adequate medical facility.

EMERGENCY MEDICAL EVACUATION

One of the most significant benefits of travel insurance is coverage for emergency medical evacuation. Suppose an attendee experiences a severe medical emergency that requires immediate attention beyond the capabilities of the ship's medical facilities. In that case, travel insurance can cover the high costs associated with airlifting the individual to the nearest appropriate medical center.

24/7 ASSISTANCE SERVICES

Allianz Travel Insurance offers 24/7 assistance services, which can be a lifeline in an emergency. Whether an attendee needs help finding a local doctor, replacing a lost passport, or arranging transportation, these services provide invaluable support, ensuring that attendees feel supported and never alone when facing a crisis.

PEACE OF MIND

Ultimately, travel insurance's most significant advantage is its peace of mind. Knowing that a safety net is in place allows attendees to focus on the conference and enjoy the experience without the constant worry of "what if" scenarios. This peace of mind can enhance the event's overall atmosphere, as attendees are more relaxed and engaged.

ALLIANZ TRAVEL INSURANCE: A TRUSTED PARTNER

Allianz Travel Insurance is a trusted name in the industry. It offers a range of plans tailored to meet different needs and budgets. Its extensive experience and commitment to customer service ensure that attendees receive the best possible protection and support.

CUSTOMIZABLE PLANS

Allianz offers customizable travel insurance plans that can be tailored to the specific needs of a corporate cruise conference. Whether providing higher coverage limits for medical expenses or adding particular protections for valuable equipment, these plans can be adjusted to ensure that all attendees feel catered to and adequately covered.

EASY CLAIMS PROCESS

Allianz's claims process is straightforward and customer-friendly. It ensures that reimbursements or claims are handled efficiently and with minimal hassle. This user-friendly approach is crucial for maintaining attendee satisfaction and guaranteeing swift resolution of any issues.

ADDITIONAL BENEFITS

Allianz Travel Insurance also offers additional benefits, such as concierge services, to enhance the travel experience. These services can assist with booking restaurant reservations, securing event tickets, or providing destination information, adding an extra layer of convenience and enjoyment for attendees.

When it comes to planning a safe and worry-free corporate cruise conference, travel insurance is a must. Allianz Travel Insurance, with its comprehensive coverage for a wide range of potential issues, provides invaluable protection and peace of mind. With Allianz, every attendee can focus on the conference and enjoy their journey, knowing they are fully protected. This peace of mind is what sets Allianz apart.

THE IMPORTANCE OF HAVING A CRUISE AND/OR TRAVEL AGENT CONTRACT FOR CORPORATE CRUISE CONFERENCES

In the realm of corporate cruise conferences, meticulous planning and execution are essential to ensure a seamless and successful event. One critical aspect of this process is securing a comprehensive Cruise and/or Travel Agent Contract. This contract, far from being a mere formality, is a foundational document that protects the company hosting the cruise conference by clearly outlining the responsibilities, expectations, and obligations of all parties involved. Below, we explore the key reasons why having such a contract is indispensable, as well as the numerous benefits it brings to the table.

CLEAR DEFINITION OF RESPONSIBILITIES

A Cruise and/or Travel Agent Contract explicitly defines the roles and responsibilities of the travel agent, the cruise line, and the hosting company. This clarity helps prevent misunderstandings and disputes. The contract specifies who is responsible for booking accommodations, arranging transportation, managing onboard activities, and handling special requests. This detailed delineation of duties is a proactive measure that helps mitigate the risk of disputes and ensures smooth coordination.

LIABILITY COVERAGE

In the event of unforeseen circumstances, such as accidents, medical emergencies, or trip cancellations, a well-drafted contract provides a safety net for the hosting company. It specifies the extent of the travel agent's and cruise line's liability, ensuring that the hosting company is not held accountable for incidents beyond its control. This protection is a crucial measure for safeguarding the company's financial and legal interests.

Cost Transparency and Payment Terms

A comprehensive contract includes detailed information about the costs associated with the cruise conference, including accommodation, meals, transportation, activities, and any additional services. It outlines the payment terms, including deposit requirements, payment schedules, and cancellation policies. This transparency helps the hosting company manage its budget effectively and avoid unexpected expenses.

Refund and Cancellation Policies

The contract clearly states the refund and cancellation policies, providing peace of mind for the hosting company. In case of cancellations or changes in the conference schedule, the contract ensures that the company is aware of any potential penalties and the conditions under which refunds are applicable. This information is vital for managing financial risks and making informed decisions.

Quality Assurance and Service Standards

The contract sets forth the performance expectations for the travel agent and the cruise line. It includes specific criteria for service quality, such as the standard of accommodations, the quality of meals, the professionalism of staff, and the availability of facilities. These benchmarks ensure that the hosting company receives the level of service promised, enhancing the overall experience for conference attendees.

CONTINGENCY PLANS AND PROBLEM RESOLUTION

A well-drafted contract includes provisions for contingency plans and problem resolution. It outlines the procedures to be followed in case of service failures, delays, or other issues. This proactive approach ensures that the hosting company can swiftly address any problems that arise, minimizing disruptions and maintaining the conference's integrity.

CUSTOMIZED ARRANGEMENTS AND SPECIAL REQUESTS

Corporate cruise conferences often require customized arrangements to meet specific needs and preferences. The contract can include clauses that detail these tailored services, such as special dietary requirements, customized itineraries, exclusive use of certain facilities, and personalized experiences. This level of customization enhances attendee satisfaction and ensures that the conference aligns with the company's vision and goals.

COORDINATION OF SPECIAL EVENTS

If the conference includes special events, such as award ceremonies, gala dinners, or team-building activities, the contract ensures that these events are meticulously planned and executed. It specifies the roles and responsibilities of the travel agent and the cruise line in coordinating these events, ensuring they meet the hosting company's expectations.

REGULATORY COMPLIANCE AND ETHICAL STANDARDS

The contract ensures all parties comply with relevant legal and regulatory requirements, including health and safety regulations, environmental standards, and consumer protection laws. This adherence is crucial for maintaining the hosting company's reputation and avoiding legal repercussions.

ETHICAL CONDUCT

The contract promotes ethical conduct by establishing clear guidelines for interactions with attendees, handling personal information, and adhering to professional standards. This commitment to ethical conduct enhances the hosting company's credibility and fosters trust among attendees.

A Cruise and/or Travel Agent Contract is a vital document that provides comprehensive protection for the company hosting a corporate cruise conference. It ensures legal protection, financial security, quality assurance, and customized arrangements while promoting regulatory compliance and ethical conduct. By clearly defining the responsibilities, expectations, and obligations of all parties involved, the contract empowers the hosting company, minimizes risks, prevents disputes, and enhances the overall success of the conference.

In the complex and dynamic environment of cruise conferences, having a robust contract is indispensable. It empowers the hosting company to confidently navigate potential challenges, ensuring a seamless and extraordinary experience for all attendees. Companies can safeguard their interests by working with experienced travel agents and legal professionals to draft a thorough and well-defined contract and focus on delivering a memorable and impactful corporate cruise conference.

8

CRUISETECH IQ: NAVIGATING COMPLEX LOGISTICS WITH CONFIDENCE AND CLARITY

I magine hosting a corporate event where the endless ocean serves as your venue, the horizon stretches as your backdrop, and every intricate detail unfolds seamlessly, orchestrated by cutting-edge technology. At the helm of this transformative experience is CruiseTech IQ, a visionary platform founded by Keith Lefkof, an expert corporate travel consultant and author of the *Cruise Retreat* trilogy, including this very book, *Navigating Brand Success*. With decades of firsthand expertise in planning corporate conferences, Keith recognized the need for a streamlined, immersive, and innovative approach to cruise event management, leading to the creation of CruiseTech IQ.

CruiseTech IQ is not just a tool; it is the bridge between the unique challenges of hosting events on a moving vessel and the art of crafting unforgettable brand experiences. Powered by the award-winning Trippus event management system with over 25 years of success in enhancing attendee engagement and improving event outcomes. CruiseTech IQ is branded as the ultimate *Cruise Conference Planning Command Center*. This platform redefines what's possible, enabling businesses to amplify their brand through seamless pre-planning, immersive on-board execution, and impactful post-event connections.

WHY CRUISETECH IQ MATTERS

Planning a cruise event is unlike any other endeavor. The confined, dynamic nature of a cruise ship demands precision, adaptability, and innovative tools to manage logistics, foster collaboration, and deliver unparalleled attendee experiences. CruiseTech IQ addresses these challenges head-on, equipping event organizers with a suite of integrated solutions designed to ensure every element of the conference flows smoothly from the first registration click to the final farewell toast on the deck.

HOW CRUISETECH IQ TRANSFORMS CRUISE EVENTS

FLAWLESS COORDINATION

CruiseTech IQ's task management suite simplifies the complexities of cruise event logistics. From scheduling workshops and allocating meeting spaces to managing AV requirements and assigning responsibilities, the platform ensures every detail aligns perfectly, even in the unique constraints of a moving venue. It's a roadmap that keeps chaos at bay, allowing organizers to focus on delivering a standout experience.

IMMERSIVE ATTENDEE ENGAGEMENT

The platform's mobile apps transform passive attendees into active participants. Personalized agendas, real-time session updates, and digital interaction tools create an environment where attendees feel seen, valued, and fully engaged. This level of customization not only heightens their experience but ensures your brand message resonates long after the ship docks.

REAL-TIME ADAPTABILITY

Cruise events are inherently dynamic, with factors like weather or technical issues demanding immediate adjustments. CruiseTech IQ's real-time coordination tools empower organizers to respond swiftly to any change, maintaining a polished and professional atmosphere no matter the circumstances.

SEAMLESS COLLABORATION

Effective event planning hinges on communication, especially when coordinating among diverse stakeholders. CruiseTech IQ facilitates this with tools that streamline task delegation, resource allocation, and ongoing collaboration. Whether you're a travel advisor, corporate organizer, or onboard coordinator, the platform fosters clarity and teamwork, ensuring the entire process feels effortless.

The CruiseTech IQ Advantage

CruiseTech IQ is a commitment to excellence in cruise conferences. By aligning your event with the luxury, adventure, and exclusivity of a cruise experience, you elevate your brand's perception and create an unforgettable journey for attendees. The platform's custom-branded websites, automated registrations, and attendee engagement tools amplify your brand's reach while making the planning process stress-free and efficient.

Whether you're planning your first cruise conference or refining your event management strategy, CruiseTech IQ is your partner in success. It empowers you to exceed expectations, transforming challenges into opportunities and logistics into seamless execution.

Set Sail With Confidence

CruiseTech IQ is the future of cruise event management, turning every moment into an opportunity to inspire, connect, and leave a lasting impression. With this innovative platform as your guide, your brand will make waves far beyond the ship's deck, creating an enduring story of excellence, connection, and impact. So, step aboard and let CruiseTech IQ take your brand to new horizons.

Committed to elevating the cruise conference experience, CruiseTech IQ strives for more efficiency, enjoyment, and impact for everyone involved. They empower organizers to exceed the expectations of their attendees, creating memorable and effective events that resonate well beyond their conclusion.

Whether you are orchestrating your inaugural cruise conference or seeking to refine your event management strategy, Cruise Tech IQ is your reliable partner in overcoming the challenges of cruise event planning.

So, set sail with confidence. With CruiseTech IQ, your brand will make waves that resonate far beyond the ship's deck, transforming every attendee's journey into an enduring story of connection, inspiration, and success.

www.cruisetechiq.com
Photo Courtsey of CruiseTech IQ

Powerful features for successful events

Everything you need for on-site events!

Invite and gather bookings

Send personal invitations and collect event registrations seamlessly. Customize the design, fields and information you require.

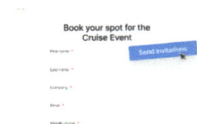

Event communication

Keep attendees updated with flexible SMS and email solutions that can be sent instantly or scheduled.

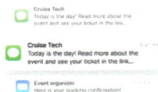

Digital tickets and checkin

No need for printing tickets! Go digital and send out your participants with digital tickets which can be scanned and validated at the event.

Event apps - the only tool participants needs

Everything for your event - gathered in one place! you collect tickets, directions, programs, interaction and much more. Customize with your graphic profile to tailor it to your event.

Gather information on a event page

Spark the interest of your event with a stunning and dedicated event page! Include the program, tickets, about the event and so much more! Design it to your liking.

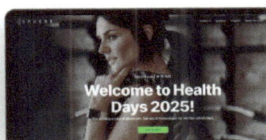

Interaction and polls

Engage with your audience by providing live polls and on-site interaction, meaning they have the option to ask and answer questions.

Lead Management

Collect and manage hot leads from events by scanning attendees QR-codes on their name badges with your mobile phone.

Table seating and group placement

Randomize or manually select people into groups or seat at a table. The participant will directly see it in their event app.

Send out survies and questionnaire

Get real-time feedback with surveys from your participants and send follow-up questionnaires.

Powerful analytics and reports

Customize your own reports or see pre-defined metrics from your event to get a better understanding of it's performance.

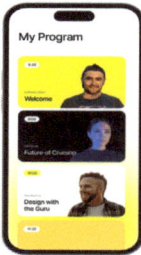

Check-in participants

5.32K

Survey

My Program

Welcome

Future of Onvarto

Design with the Guru

Enhance Engagement and Connectivity with Our Event App

Attendees benefit from our platform's mobile apps, which provide access to personalized agendas, real-time notifications about sessions or venue changes, and digital interaction with other participants and speakers. This engagement level not only enhances their experience but also fosters greater involvement with the conference's offerings.

9

ONBOARD BRILLIANCE: ELEVATING BRAND PRESENCE WITH A CUSTOMIZABLE EVENT TECH APP

In today's event landscape, branding is more than just logos and banners; it's about weaving a brand's essence into every touchpoint and every interaction, especially within digital spaces. When hosting a conference on a cruise ship, a dedicated event app can transform the attendee experience, turning each moment into a branded encounter. At the forefront of this shift is CruiseTech IQ, a powerful white-label app that uniquely focuses on amplifying branding opportunities, maximizing sponsor visibility, and enhancing attendee engagement. Its ability to transform the attendee experience is unparalleled, making it the ultimate choice for event organizers in the cruise industry.

More than just a functional tool, CruiseTech IQ seamlessly becomes a digital extension of the event itself. From the moment attendees download the app, they're welcomed into a branded digital space that mirrors the conference's look and feel. Every color, logo, and interface is customized to match the brand's identity, creating a cohesive visual journey that reinforces the event's purpose. This immersion transforms the app into a portable conference environment, with attendees consistently connected to the brand message throughout their journey. With branded screens, custom homepages, and seamless design elements, CruiseTech IQ ensures that branding is part of every interaction, guiding attendees smoothly from pre-event registration to post-event follow-up.

CruiseTech IQ also redefines how sponsors engage with attendees, making achieving high-impact visibility through integrated features easy. Each time an attendee opens the app, sponsors have the chance to make an impression with splash screens, logos, or personalized messages. CruiseTech IQ's layout includes sponsor profiles, content hubs, and dedicated spaces where sponsors can showcase multimedia content, from videos and brochures to links and interactive product displays. These virtual showrooms offer sponsors a dynamic way to connect with attendees beyond a physical booth, establishing a more personal, engaging, and immersive presence.

The app's interactive features further elevate sponsor engagement, providing opportunities for direct interaction through live polls, surveys, and Q&A sessions.

Imagine a sponsor launching a poll related to a new product or service, allowing attendees to weigh in and offer instant feedback, or hosting a Q&A session about industry trends where attendees can engage directly with sponsor representatives. These features foster direct interaction between sponsors and attendees, building rapport and increasing brand affinity. Push notifications also enhance real-time engagement, enabling sponsors to send updates about exclusive sessions, workshops, or special offers, ensuring they remain visible and top-of-mind.

Gamification adds an additional layer of engagement. Through CruiseTech IQ, sponsors can set up scavenger hunts, challenges, or quizzes that encourage attendees to explore their brand interactively. By incentivizing participation, such as earning points for visiting a sponsor booth or joining a session, sponsors can drive more traffic and interest, creating memorable and fun experiences for attendees while boosting their visibility.

One of the hallmarks of CruiseTech IQ is its ability to deliver personalized experiences that make each attendee's journey unique. Engagement is further amplified through interactive features like polls, surveys, and live Q&A sessions. For instance, a sponsor might host a poll tied to a product launch or lead a Q&A session on emerging industry trends. These features foster direct interaction between sponsors and attendees, building rapport and increasing brand affinity. The personalization features of CruiseTech IQ empower event organizers to cater to their attendees' individual needs, enhancing their overall experience.

Gamification is also a powerful way to engage attendees while enhancing sponsor visibility. The app can integrate features like challenges, scavenger hunts, or quizzes to encourage attendees to interact with sponsor content. Attendees might earn points for visiting sponsor booths or participating in sponsored sessions, which can be redeemed for prizes. This creates a fun and engaging experience that drives more traffic and interest to sponsor profiles.

During the cruise, the app functions as a digital concierge, keeping attendees informed, connected, and engaged. After the conference ends, the app remains a valuable resource, hosting recorded sessions, downloadable materials, and follow-up content. Sponsors can continue engaging with attendees by sharing follow-up resources, exclusive offers, and invitations to future events, fostering a lasting connection and maximizing brand retention. The convenience and ease of use of CruiseTech IQ ensure that event organizers can rely on it to deliver a seamless and engaging experience for their attendees.

A white-label app offers complete control over branding, ensuring a consistent and immersive experience that reinforces brand identity at every stage of the attendee journey. Every interaction, from the splash screen to the final goodbye message, reflects the event's branding, creating a cohesive experience that strengthens the company's message. Attendees can view introductions to keynote speakers, explore exclusive activities, and receive notifications about sponsor-led giveaways, familiarizing them with the app and increasing pre-event engagement. The control over branding that CruiseTech IQ offers empowers event organizers to create a cohesive and immersive experience that resonates with their attendees.

This level of customization extends to the app's overall design, which can be themed to match the look and feel of the cruise conference, whether it's a sleek, modern design for a tech-focused summit or an elegant, timeless style for a luxury industry gathering. Sponsors also benefit from this cohesive, professional environment, as their branding is seamlessly integrated into the app, enhancing visibility without feeling intrusive.

With CruiseTech IQ at the heart of your event, branding takes on a new dimension, turning a traditional conference into an immersive, memorable journey that captivates attendees and strengthens connections.

This powerful, white-label app redefines how brands and sponsors engage, offering a seamless blend of logistics, personalized interaction, and continuous engagement that resonates long after the cruise has ended. Designed specifically for cruise-based conferences, CruiseTech IQ is the ultimate tool for those looking to amplify their brand impact and elevate the attendee experience, making it the cruise conference app of choice for unforgettable events.

CONCLUSION: SETTING SAIL TOWARD YOUR BRAND'S FUTURE

As you reach the final pages of *Navigating Brand Success*, you now have the tools, insights, and inspiration to elevate your brand through transformative, memorable events. The journey we've taken together highlights the unparalleled opportunities that cruise-based corporate gatherings provide unique environments where connections deepen, loyalty strengthens, and a brand's story truly comes to life.

Luxury cruise ships offer more than a venue; they provide a stage for innovation, elegance, and engagement. Whether hosting a leadership retreat, client appreciation event, or company-wide conference, these settings allow brands to showcase their identity in ways that traditional venues cannot match. From the grandeur of iconic liners like Cunard to the immersive experiences made possible by CruiseTech IQ, you can create unforgettable events that resonate long after disembarkation.

Imagine the ripple effects of bringing your brand to life at sea: employees more aligned with your mission, clients more connected to your vision, and stakeholders inspired by the creativity and thoughtfulness of your approach. With up to 30% in event cost savings and the added value of all-inclusive luxury, the ROI speaks for itself not just in financial terms but in the lasting impressions and deeper connections formed.

The strategies outlined in this book have been designed to empower corporate leaders, brand strategists, and event planners to reimagine their approach to brand building. By blending the practical with the extraordinary, you can turn events into tools for growth, differentiation, and lasting success. From leveraging the storytelling power of breathtaking destinations to crafting personalized attendee journeys, you are now equipped to transform your brand's potential into a future filled with success.

But this is just the beginning. The world of cruise-based events is dynamic, filled with untapped possibilities waiting for bold brands ready to set sail. To take the next step, reach out to explore how we can help you bring these ideas to life. Whether it's a consultation, access to CruiseTech IQ, or partnering with us to design your next unforgettable event, we offer expertise, resources, and a commitment to excellence. We're here to guide you every step of the way.

Now, it's time to act. Transform your corporate events from routine gatherings into inspiring journeys. Let your brand stand out in the competitive sea of business. Connect with us today and set your course for a new level of success. The horizon is yours are you ready to navigate it? The next step is in your hands, and we're here to help you take it.

Ready to Explore Your Next Unforgettable
Cruise Conference?
Schedule a complimentary 15-minute consultation
call with us today!

Cruise Planners – Land N Sea Trips
www.LandNSeaTrips.com

Discover How Cruisetech IQ Can Elevate
Your Cruise Planning!
Schedule your complimentary 15-minute
demo call with us today!

www.CruiseTechIQ.com

Sign up now to download our exclusive
Supplemental Cruise Conference Checklists and get
to know author Keith Lefkof!

www.CruiseRetreatBooks.com

ABOUT THE AUTHOR

Keith's unique blend of experience in the travel industry and corporate America, spanning over two decades, sets him apart as a visionary force. His rich background includes luxury and corporate travel consulting, hospitality management, corporate real estate, franchise consulting, and entrepreneurship. This diverse expertise empowers Keith to craft compelling narratives and impactful solutions, as demonstrated in his groundbreaking book Navigating Brand Success.

As a franchise owner of a full-service travel agency and a proud franchisee of Cruise Planners, an internationally acclaimed and award-winning brand, Keith harnesses its global reach, cutting-edge technology, and unmatched expertise to curate unforgettable experiences. Whether designing seamless family getaways or orchestrating transformative corporate cruise conferences, Keith's unwavering dedication to service, innovation, and value sets him apart. His team of travel and event professionals takes a tech-savvy yet deeply personal approach, ensuring every cruise event is both memorable and meaningful.

Keith embarks on a transformative literary journey with his groundbreaking trilogy of B2B books. The series redefines the untapped potential of corporate cruises as a powerful engine for business success. Each book in the series is a beacon of innovation, offering actionable insights and transformative strategies for organizations ready to elevate their game.

The journey begins with *Navigating Brand Success*, a compelling guide that explores the untapped potential of cruise events to amplify company growth and strengthen brand identity. By weaving immersive travel into the fabric of brand strategy, this book reveals how to create experiences that resonate deeply with clients and stakeholders, sparking optimism and hope for the future. Next, *Corporate Conferences at Sea serves* as both a masterclass and a practical workbook. It equips leaders with the tools to transform traditional meetings into extraordinary, impactful events. The trilogy culminates with *Cruising to Success*, which delves into the transformative power of coaching and leadership retreats aboard cruises, providing practical advice that can be implemented in any business setting.

Together, these three books are essential reading for forward-thinking companies eager to harness the magic of the open sea to amplify their brand, foster authentic connections, and achieve meaningful business outcomes. Keith's trilogy is more than a guide; it's an invitation to reimagine what's possible when business and travel converge, sparking new ideas and strategies.

Keith's innovative spirit extends to technology with the launch of CruiseTech IQ, a cutting-edge event management platform developed in partnership with the award-winning Trippus event management company. Designed to revolutionize cruise events and conferences, CruiseTech IQ sets new standards for planning, collaboration, engagement, and execution, cementing Keith's role as a trailblazer in the industry.

Beyond his professional achievements, Keith finds balance in his personal life. Residing in Boca Raton, Florida, with his family, he is also an accomplished Ironman and marathon finisher, embodying the discipline and endurance that define his professional and personal pursuits. Keith's journey is one of innovation, service, and relentless passion, a testament to his belief in the power of travel to transform lives and businesses.